Which Ad
Pulled Best?

McGraw-Hill/Irwin Series in Marketing

ii

Which Ad Pulled Best?

Ninth Edition

40 Case Histories on How to Write and Design Ads That Work

Scott C. Purvis
President, Gallup & Robinson, Inc.

Philip Ward Burton
Indiana University

McGraw-Hill
Irwin

Boston   Burr Ridge, IL   Dubuque, IA   Madison, WI   New York
San Francisco   St. Louis   Bangkok   Bogotá   Caracas   Kuala Lumpur
Lisbon   London   Madrid   Mexico City   Milan   Montreal   New Delhi
Santiago   Seoul   Singapore   Sydney   Taipei   Toronto

McGraw-Hill Higher Education &

A Division of The **McGraw-Hill** *Companies*

WHICH AD PULLED BEST?

Published by McGraw-Hill/Irwin, a business unit of The McGraw-Hill Companies, Inc., 1221 Avenue of the Americas, New York,, NY, 10020. Copyright © 2003 by The McGraw-Hill Companies, Inc. All rights reserved. No part of this publication may be reproduced or distributed in any form or by any means, or stored in a database or retrieval system, without the prior written consent of The McGraw-Hill Companies, Inc., including, but not limited to, in any network or other electronic storage or transmission, or broadcast for distance learning. Some ancillaries, including electronic and print components, may not be available to customers outside the United States.

This book is printed on acid-free paper.

1 2 3 4 5 6 7 8 9 0 CUS/CUS 0 9 8 7 6 5 4 3 2

ISBN   0-07-255664-1

Publisher: *John E. Biernat*
Executive editor: *Linda Schreiber*
Editorial coordinator: *Sarah Crago*
Marketing manager: *Kimberly Kanakes*
Media producer: *Craig Atkins*
Senior project manager: *Kari Geltemeyer*
Production supervisor: *Gina Hangos*
Senior designer: *Pam Verros*
Photo research coordinator: *Kathy Shive*
Supplement producer: *Matthew Perry*
Senior digital content specialist: *Brian Nacik*
Cover and interior designer: *Pam Verros*
Typeface: *10/12 Times New Roman*
Compositor: *GAC Indianapolis*
Printer: *Von Hoffmann Graphics*

Library of Congress Cataloging-in-Publication Data

Which ad pulled best? : 40 case histories on how to write and design ads that work /
[edited by] Scott C. Purvis, Philip Ward Burton.-- 9th ed.
        p. cm. -- (McGraw-Hill/Irwin series in marketing)
    Includes index.
    ISBN 0-07-255664-1 (alk. paper)
    1. Advertising. 2. Advertising copy--Evaluation. I. Purvis, Scott C. II. Burton, Philip
Ward, 1910-III. Series.
HF5823.W467 2003
659.1--dc21

                                                                2002026342

www.mhhe.com

Contents

Foreword

What kind of advertising copy and illustrations get the best results? Whether you're a practitioner or a student of advertising and marketing, you'll have opinions based upon experience, common sense, intuition, and sheer guesswork. Sometimes these opinions help, and sometimes they don't.

To help you in creative evaluation, this book shows you, through tested advertising, what elements were responsible for their performance. When you see in example after example that certain principles work most of the time, you will begin to rely less on guesswork and intuition and more on these guiding doctrines. You'll learn some of the success factors that increase the pulling power of advertisements. You'll see advertising techniques that attract attention, create interest, arouse desire, and stimulate action.

Scott Purvis edited this new edition and all the critical analyses in the accompanying *Instructor's Manual.* Mr. Purvis is ideally qualified for this work through his years of experience as a practitioner working with many of the leading companies and agencies.

The author also wishes to note the passing of Philip Ward Burton, professor in the School of Journalism, Indiana University, who initially developed the book and was co-author for so many years . . . outstanding educator, impassioned practitioner, gentleman, and friend.

The author wishes to thank William H. Van Pelt, Jr., for his contribution to this book and his tireless work in selecting the ad pairs and presenting their interesting stories.

The ninth edition of this popular book fits admirably into the list of books we offer practitioners, teachers, and students of advertising. Most of all, it brings real-life experiences to the classroom.

Scott Purvis   *The Editors*
Author   McGraw Hill Books

Consumer Advertisements Tested by Gallup & Robinson

EXAMPLE	11	12	13	14	15
Page	61	63	65	67	69
Advertiser(s)	Dove Olay	York	Silk Soy Milk	Benadryl	Hugo Gucci
Product or Service	Body Wash	Candy	Dairy	Medicine	Cologne
Publication(s) Used	*Ladies' Home Journal* *People*	*People* *Parents*	*People*	*People* *Ladies' Home Journal*	*GQ*

Influencing Factors	Product uniqueness
	Product focus
	Disjointed layout
	Direct/indirect headlines
		Product focus
		Concept imagery
		Playfulness
		Mental work
			Humor
			Subtlety
			Simple, direct layout
				Direct headline
				Product at point
				  of focus
				Stereotype
				  illustration/unusual
				  perspective
					Brand identification
					Lack of reader
					  orientation
					Nonintegrated
					  elements
					Vague illustration

EXAMPLE	16	17	18	19	20
Page	71	73	75	77	79
Advertiser(s)	Kleenex	Dannon Breyers	Kraft	Timex	Glad Ziploc
Product or Service	Tissues	Yogurt	Salad Dressing	Watches	Storage Bags
Publication(s) Used	*Ladies' Home Journal* *People*	*People* *Ladies' Home Journal*	*Glamour* *People*	*GQ* *People*	*Bon Appetit* *Ladies' Home Journal*

Influencing Factors	Direct, benefit headline
	Product focus
	Clear, benefit copy
	Indirection
	Mental work
		Attention-getting
		  illustrations can
		  overwhelm product
		  (competing interest)
		Taste appeal
		Brand identification
			Playfulness
			Indirection
			Unusual/static
			  illustrations
			Variety
				Variety
				Identification
				Uniqueness lost
				Need for integration
					Visual comparison
					Demonstration
					Identification
					Confusing illustration
					Say-nothing headline

EXAMPLE	21	22	23	24	25
Page	81	83	85	87	89
Advertiser(s)	Viagra	Huggies Pampers	Scope	Tampax	Nivea Ponds
Product of Service	Prescription Medicine	Diapers	Mouthwash	Tampons	Make-up remover
Publication(s) Used	*Ladies' Home Journal* *People*	*People* *Parents*	*Glamour* *Cosmopolitan* *Parents*	*Glamour* *Cosmopolitan* *People*	*Allure* *Ladies' Home Journal* *Glamour* *People*

Influencing Factors	Light tough disarms heavy
	  subject
	Holiday tie-in
	Encourage reader
	  involvement
		Fantasy
		Mental work
		Problem solution
		Orient reader to topic
		Mood can enhance
		  reaction
		Distinctive illustration
			Alliteration; clear
			  headlines
			Concept imagery
				Ad oriented
				  rather than
				  reader oriented
				Symbolism
				Distinctive
				  illustration
				Brand
				  identification
				Benefit should
				  be explicit
					Stereotyped
					  illustration
					Lack of reader
					  orientation
					Linking ad elements
					Proof-positive
					  demonstration
					Copy easy, inviting

EXAMPLE	26	27	28	29	30
page	91	93	95	97	99
Advertiser(s)	Suave Secret	Ivory Dial	Willow Lake White Rain	Wedding Channel.com	Miracle Whip
Product or Service	Deodorant	Soap	Shampoo	Computer Online Services	Salad Dressing
Publication(s) Used	*People* *Parents*	*Glamour* *Ladies's Home Journal*	*Glamour* *People*	*Glamour* *People*	*Ladies' Home Journal* *People*
Influencing Factors	Direct headline Strong product identification Dynamic/static illustrations	Stereotyped illustration Involve the reader The mood that charms	Beware of being too subtle or passive Overlooked copy Illustration should stop the reader and orient to topic/brand Persuasion often needs more than just brand memorability	Fantasy and mental work Indirection Orient reader to topic	Link ad elements Product focus Humor Celebrity power

EXAMPLE	31	32	33	34	35
Page	101	103	105	107	109
Advertiser(s)	Jell-O	Lily of France Barely There	Aussie Head & Shoulders	Nexcare Johnson & Johnson	Asics Skechers
Product or Service	Gelatin	Lingerie	Haircare	Bandages	Athletic Shoes
Publication(s) Used	*People* *Ladies' Home Journal*	*People* *Ladies' Home Journal*	*GQ*	*People* *Parents*	*People* *Allure*
Influencing Factors	Larger-than life illustration Product focus Concept imagery News Clear, benefit headline Visual pun—indirection Brand identification	Demonstration Tone: don't come to the ball in your sneakers Identification	Indirection Weak headline	Don't obscure product/topic Identification Problem/solution Link ad elements	Orient reader to topic Misdirecting Identification Hard-to-read/irrelevant copy Variety/demonstration

EXAMPLE	36	37	38	39	40
Page	111	113	115	117	119
Advertiser(s)	Avon Lipstick Almay Lipstick	Smart Start	DuPont Wamsutta	Maxwell House General Foods	Russell Stover
Product or Service	Make-up	Cereal	Bed Linens	Coffee	Candy
Publication(s) Used	*People* *Parents*	*People*	*Ladies' Home Journal* *People*	*People* *Ladies' Home Journal*	*People*
Influencing Factors	Giantism Variety Clear, benefit, easy-to-read copy Stereotype	Mood Borrowed interest Obscure illustration	Stereotype happy people Product focus Indirection	Mood Headline Linking of elements	Say-little ad Visual comparison News Concept imagery Call-outs Linking of elements

Principles Demonstrated by Tested Advertisements

Example Number

Copy
(appeals, ideas, subject matter, technique)

1, 2, 3, 4, 9, 16, 24, 25, 28, 29, 31, 35, 36, 38

Headlines
(importance, techniques, faults, appeals used)

1, 2, 3, 5, 6, 7, 8, 10, 11, 14, 16, 18, 20, 22, 23, 26, 33, 39, 40

Layout, illustration, typography
(influence, techniques, subject matter, importance, suitability)

1, 2, 3, 4, 5, 6, 7, 9, 10, 11, 12, 13, 14, 15, 17, 18, 20, 21, 22, 23, 24, 25, 26, 27, 28, 29, 30, 31, 32, 33, 34, 35, 36, 37, 38

Organization of advertisement
(unity, strong theme, tie-in of elements, devices to attract and hold interest)

2, 4, 5, 9, 11, 13, 18, 19, 20, 21, 22, 24, 25, 26, 28, 29, 30, 32, 34, 39, 40

Product or service
(importance to readers, identification of, focus on product and/or advertisers)

1, 3, 4, 6, 7, 8, 9, 11, 12, 14, 15, 16, 17, 19, 26, 31, 34, 35, 38, 40

List of Advertisers

*Example number(s) in boldface.

Which Ad
Pulled Best?

The Who-What-How of Testing Printed Advertising

The 40 pairs of advertisements you will find in this book were tested by the prominent research organization, Gallup & Robinson. They are real ads, tested as part of an actual research program, and the lessons that are drawn are also real. In the following material you will learn the methodology employed in the testing. Next, you will learn the research techniques used by two other well-known research organizations, Readex and Starch. This will familiarize you with other types of methods that are used. In addition, there will be a general discussion of research, various methodologies, criticisms and virtues, and finally, guidelines for advertisers and agencies that stem from research findings.

ADVERTISING RESEARCH IS A RELATIVE NEWCOMER

In the early days of advertising there was almost no research—keeping records of inquiries produced by advertisements was about it. Then came the depression, when cost-conscious advertisers demanded to know the factors behind the success or failure of advertisements. Thus, you might say that meaningful scientific research began in the 1930s.

Advertising research has been controversial from the start. It is *still* the subject of debate among advertisers, advertising agency people, and researchers themselves; there is no system on which all agree. Still, many areas of guesswork for the early advertisers have been eliminated. From research, we now have guidelines that, if followed, give advertisers much more assurance of obtaining good readership, communication, inquiries, and/or sales.

Today advertising research is used by most leading advertisers and is well integrated into the business processes they use for managing their advertising investment and making it more effective.

GALLUP & ROBINSON METHODOLOGY

Gallup & Robinson pioneered many of the research techniques that have become standard for helping advertisers and agencies evaluate the effectiveness of their advertising in the marketplace and gain a better understanding of the advertising process. The systems have been used to evaluate over 120,000 print ads and 60,000 television commercials.

The examples that are used in this book were tested under Gallup & Robinson's Magazine Impact Research Service (MIRS). Its specific objective is to assess in-market performance of individual ads or campaigns relative to previous history and the performance of the competition within specific industries or product categories.

To accomplish this objective, the MIRS system permits users to assess their own and competitive advertising in the context of actual consumer and business magazines either as the ad naturally appears or as it has been tipped into a test issue. The sample size for a typical consumer survey is approximately 150 men and/or women, ages 18 and older. Qualified readers are located by continuous household canvass in 10 metropolitan areas geographically dispersed across the United States. Respondents qualify by having read two of the last four issues of the test magazine or others in the same classification, but they must not have read the current issue.

The test magazine is placed at the respondent's home, and the respondent is interviewed by telephone the following day. Readers are given no advance information of the nature of the interview but are requested to read the magazine on the day of placement and not to read it on the day of the interview.

During the telephone interview, respondents are asked preliminary questions to determine readership. A list of ads appearing in the magazine is read, and respondents are asked which ad they remember. For each ad the respondent claims to recall, he or she is asked a series of open- and closed-ended questions. These are called the impact questions and include:

1. You may be familiar with other ads for _____, but thinking only of this issue, please describe the ad as you remember it. What did the ad look like and say?

2. What sales points or reasons for buying did they show or talk about?

3. What did you learn about the (product/service) from this ad?

4. What thoughts and feelings went through your mind when you looked at the ad?

5. The advertiser tried to increase your interest in his (product/service). How was your buying interest affected?

- Increased considerably
- Increased somewhat
- Not affected
- Decreased somewhat
- Decreased considerably

6. What was in the ad that makes you say that?

The impact questions yield a rich quality of verbatim testimony that is used to produce three basic measurements of advertising effectiveness.

1. *Intrusiveness (Proved Name Registration)*—the percentage of respondents who can accurately describe the ad the day following exposure. This measure is an indicator of the ad's ability to command attention. For comparative purposes, the percentages are adjusted for space/color unit cost and issue level.

2. *Idea communication*—the distribution of respondents' descriptions of the ad's selling propositions and of their reactions to the ad. This measure is an indicator of what ideas and feelings are communicated by the ad.

3. *Persuasion (Favorable Buying Attitude)*—the distribution of respondent statements of how the ad affected purchase interest. This measure is a relative indicator of the ad's ability to persuade. For corporate advertising, the persuasion measure indicates the extent to which the ad made a strong case for the advertiser.

In addition, a series of special questions about how people react to the advertising itself and to the brand is also asked of people who remember the ad or who do not remember it but were reexposed to it during the interview. Each interview concludes with a series of classification questions.

Because different product categories have different interest levels the norms of performance can vary by category. For this reason, Gallup & Robinson uses category-specific norms. The extensive coverage of MIRS provides a wide range of sex-specific, normative data for most product groups.

Each ad impact report on client and/or competitive advertisements contains the following:

- Copy of the tested ad.
- Intrusiveness (proved name registration) measure.
- Idea communication profile.
- Persuasion (favorable buying attitude) measure.
- Standard and customized evaluative and diagnostic measures.
- Norms.
- Verbatim testimony for the ad.
- Sample characteristics.

MIRS also allows for testing an ad that is not published in an MIRS schedule magazine. The advertiser may tip into a test issue so that the test ad appears as if it ran naturally. The technique is useful for pretesting an ad or for providing extra posttest opportunities.

In addition to diagnostic information that explains how performance can be improved, the MIRS system yields evaluative measures of intrusiveness (recall) and persuasion. Intrusiveness is measured by Proved Name Registration (PNR) and is the ability of the ad to stop and hold the audience's attention to the advertiser's name. Persuasion is measured by Favorable Buying Attitude (FBA) and is the ability of the ad to increase buying interest or generate favor for the product, service, or idea. It is important to note that intrusiveness and persuasion are not correlated with each other.

READEX READER INTEREST STUDIES

Readex, an independent mail survey research firm, has been designing and conducting readership research for print communications since 1947. The firm conducts about 400 studies per year for over 240 different publications.

Readex offers three off-the-shelf readership studies: Red Sticker II™, MESSAGE IMPACT®, and Ad Perception™.

Red Sticker II is closest to a "classical" ad readership study. It provides measurement of both ads and editorial. This study asks readers three questions of each item studied: Did you see it? Did you read it? Did you find it of interest? "Interest" in advertising is considered, by Readex, to be a fundamental element in the selling process. The firm says that to sell a product or service a prospective customer must first be made aware of the opportunity (seeing), and sufficient interest must then be developed (reading) to motivate the prospect toward the sale. "Interest" equals a considered opinion of the material seen and read.

MESSAGE IMPACT is a more in-depth study that combines qualitative readership dimensions. This study type is designed to answer the questions most often asked by advertisers and agencies.

- Ratings for an ad's stopping power are calculated. Readers are asked to rate an ad on attention-getting ability, believability, and information value.

- Readers are asked to list action taken or planned as a result of seeing the ad or offer feedback on their impressions of a company's image.

- A transcript of verbatim comments is provided, including comments on the ad's message, the feeling the reader received from the advertisement, or the reader's perceived image of the company.

Ad Perception provides quantitative feedback on the three basic elements of effective ads. Readers evaluate each ad by indicating whether or not the ad was attention getting, believable, and informative. The attention-getting score refers to the visual stopping power of the ad. The other two scores (believability and information value) refer to the message found in the copy of the ad. A successful ad is usually believable (credible) as well as informative (in terms of specifications, applications, etc.).

Results for each of the above study types are published in readership study reports, usually available three to five weeks after the study closes.

Reports for Red Sticker II and Ad Perception are broken into several sections. First is information on the purpose and method. This is followed by a traffic flow-chart, a list of high scoring ads, scores for size/color categories, scores for product/service categories, and graphical presentations of historical averages for both size/color as well as product/service.

For MESSAGE IMPACT, reports have four sections of information: purpose and method; reader ratings ("This ad" compared to averages for product/service and size/color categories); reader actions ("this ad" compared to averages for product/service and size/color categories); and reader verbatim comments.

Readex has chosen to specialize in surveys through the mail. A readership survey mailing usually consists of (1) an alert letter, (2) a survey kit that includes a cover letter with a questionnaire *or* a duplicate copy of the study issue, plus a business reply envelope, and (3) a reminder mailing. Completed surveys are returned to Readex for processing.

Advantages of the Readex methodology are:

1. Lowest cost per completed interview among all survey methods.

2. Suitable for large samples.

3. Large geographic scope plus geographically representative.

4. Eliminates interviewer bias.

5. Respondents answer at their convenience; allows more time to answer thought-provoking or technical questions.

6. Encourages candid responses by assuring anonymity.

ROPER STARCH WORLDWIDE, INC.

For many years the Starch advertisement readership service has been used widely by a variety of advertisers. Because the Starch service uses recognition testing, this means that respondents are asked what they actually read in a publication instead of what they "usually" read.

In conducting the research, Starch interviewers first qualify respondents as having read the publication used for test purposes. After this, they check the advertisement reading of the respondents. When all the interviews are completed, the results are totaled and readers are put into one of three categories.

1. *Noted.* These are respondents who have merely remembered seeing the advertisement but can't identify the product or advertiser.

2. *Advertiser associated.* In this case, the readers have seen the advertisement and have read enough to be able to identify the product and/or advertiser.

3. *Read most.* Here the readers have read 50 percent or more of the advertisement's reading matter.

As part of the service, Starch provides cost ratios of the advertisements and ranks them in terms of the dollars expended to obtain readers. An advertiser can find out how much it costs to merely get an advertisement seen, seen and associated, or read most. These figures have different meanings for different advertisers. For instance, a soft-drink advertiser who uses little body copy is more interested in advertiser associated than read most, but the advertiser of an expensive automobile might want to achieve a high read-most figure.

MOTIVATIONAL RESEARCH

Motivational research utilizes a series of free-flowing conversations by typical consumers in the course of which they hopefully will express their true feelings about the service or product being investigated. Such a report may describe the kinds of associations engendered. These might be obtained through psychological testing that uses projective techniques such as free word association, sentence completion, or picture responses.

Out of the foregoing will come analyses of what the findings mean to advertisers, because interpretations must be furnished to explain the significance of consumers' stream-of-consciousness conversations or the associations discovered in administering the tests.

Motivational research investigators usually proceed on the assumption that they do not know what their research may uncover, because irrational or subrational behavior, drives, fears, and desires may lie behind people's reactions to the product or situation being studied. Out of the study may come reasons that respondents could give the ordinary researcher, but probably will not.

Most motivational research is concerned with the subconscious or preconscious level and has been prompted by the feeling that asking people directly how they feel about something will fail to uncover how they really feel underneath. Although motivational research—or MR, as it is known—is still practiced, it is no longer the fad it once was when the advertising industry thought it provided a sure formula for creative success. However, many of today's focus groups use methods that flow from this work.

INQUIRY TESTING

Inquiry tests are made by keeping track of the number of inquires produced by each advertisement. For example, an advertiser offers something free, or at nominal cost, and then sees how many people are interested enough to follow up on the offer. A second advertisement making the same offer will then be run and resulting inquiries counted. The results from the two advertisements can then be compared on the basis of inquiries produced.

In order to be certain that results come from a specific advertisement, the advertiser inserts a key number in the coupon, or in a paragraph near the bottom of the advertisement in which the offer appears, and suggests that respondents write in to take advantage of the offer. "Keys" have taken many forms, such as a post office box number, a street address, a room number in an office building, or a telephone number, and can be changed each time a different advertisement is run.

Inquiries are sorted according to the advertisement that produced them as they come in. Records are kept of how many inquiries are produced by each advertisement run in each different publication. Such records show not only which advertisements are producing the most inquiries, but also which publications.

In the case of direct mail advertising, a record can also show which inquiries are most valuable in developing sales. When mail order advertisers get an inquiry (say, a request for a catalog), they follow up with literature designed to make a sale. Then, as sales are made, they relate the number and size of orders back to the inquiry and the advertisement that made the first contact. In this way, mail order advertisers keep track not only of which advertisements produce the most inquiries, but also which locate the best prospects—quite often there is a difference.

Although sales don't necessarily match inquiry returns, and inquiries alone don't say much about the far greater percentage of people who saw but did not respond to the ad, such returns can be a good indication of the interest developed by a given advertisement. Comparisons of inquiries produced by different advertisements also indicate the relative interest created by each. This is especially true if some qualifying device is used in an advertisement, such as requiring people asking for the booklet, sample, or whatever to pay out some amount—anywhere from a few cents to several dollars—in order to obtain the offer. Such a requirement tends to discourage those not truly interested.

An advertisement itself can be a qualifying device. If it delves deeply into the subject of the merchandise for sale, it is likely that only firm prospects will read the whole advertisement down to the point where the offer is made. Then there are those advertisements that contain "buried" offers, the kind made in the middle of the body text. In this case, no coupon will be included in the advertisement.

SALES TESTS

For many advertisers, even those not in the mail order business, sales provide the real test of effectiveness. Publishers, for example, have found it profitable to sell directly through published advertising, and a number of products elicit sales directly through long television commercials. Additionally, with today's data capture capabilities at supermarkets, companies are increasingly able to see the sales consequences of their advertising.

COPY TESTING IS NOT INFALLIBLE

Like all research, errors occur in copy testing because there are so many variables that throw off results. Here are some possible problems affecting test validity.

1. Differences in the publications used.

2. Differences in page locations in the publications used (despite some experts' claims that page location is unimportant).

3. Variations in reading habits, inquiry mood, and buying activity at different times of the year.

4. Natural variations resulting simply from the law of averages.

5. Differences in the general interest in the product or service offered. This can vary among different products in a line or for the same products at different times of the year.

If all these factors are present in a copy test, results can differ widely without the copy being changed. Thus, the more these factors are kept constant between two ad studies, the more valid the comparison. Eliminating all variables from copy tests is almost impossible—no matter how ingenious the testing method, some variance is always possible—so controlling for them is important.

GUIDELINES FOR COPY REVEALED BY COPY TESTING

As you will hear over and over again, no single formula works successfully all the time in creating advertisements. Indeed the challenge is how not to become conventional and stereotypical while still being accessible.

The general guidelines that copy testing have given rise to simply indicate what has worked in the past and what is most *likely* to work in the future. If heeded by the person writing copy, the principles stemming from generalities may result in techniques and approaches that will be more right than wrong.

Following are some of the guidelines suggested by copy testing.

1. *Offer a major benefit.* Benefits take different forms—a product most people want; a product easy to get; a product worth paying for; a product priced as low as possible.

2. *Make it easy to see and read.* Despite all the findings of copy testing, this advice is frequently ignored, even by the most sophisticated advertisers and advertising agencies. Picture the benefit clearly, simply, and as large as possible. It should be presented with easy-to-grasp language—simple, convincing prose supported by a layout that is easy to follow.

3. *Establish audience identity.* Make it easy for viewers to see themselves in pictures on the screen or in illustrations in the publication. The copy, too, should involve the audience by giving ideas on how to use or profit from the benefit. In short, establish a relationship between the audience and the benefit.

4. *Attract by being new.* Advertising's strongest weapon is news—new products, new uses for products, new benefits. Accordingly, the most powerful advertisements include something novel in the benefit that offers new reasons to buy. Even old ideas presented in a new way can be compelling. Successful advertisements fit the news approach by using action pictures, modern settings, active language written in present tense, and word pictures.

5. *Be believable.* Sadly enough, when different vocations are rated according to honesty and credibility, advertising people are rated near or at the bottom. Brag and boast copy and extravagant and slick copywriter phrases are primarily responsible for this perception. To achieve believability, don't make unreasonable claims. Avoid the blue-sky approach in describing benefits. Supply proof for claims. In pictures and illustrations, show the product realistically; don't doctor it so that there is a difference between the product in the advertising and that in the hand. This same observation also holds for what you say in the copy.

6. *Stress what is unique.* Advertising people express uniqueness as a "point of difference" or

"USP"—unique selling proposition. Both terms refer to an attractive feature available solely in the advertised product and/or promoted as an exclusive benefit. The difference could be tangible, such as performance styling, price, size, or ease of use, or intangible, such as how the product might be perceived by others. Any experienced copywriter, when asked to write about a product or service, will ask: "What's different about it?" That is the starting point of the creative process.

7. *Be fresh.* Even more than being creative, an ad should be fresh. People tire of seeing the same stale stories, images, or techniques. Merely being fresh, however, without any of the above is wasted.

8. *Reward the reader for his or her time.* Whether it is new learning, reinforced conviction, or some form of purposeful entertainment, the person should feel rewarded for the time spent with your ad. That will enhance how people think of you and leave them more open to future messages.

What you have read in the foregoing only touches upon the generalities stemming from copy research. Still, each of these points is important and, if followed, will help you avoid some of the most common mistakes in writing copy. Remember though, more than any of the mechanical elements of an ad, what matters most is its creative whole.

It's the Benefit: Analysis of Which Ad Pulled Best? Examples Reveal How to Make Advertisements Pull Better

The more impressive the benefit, the greater the result in advertising. That is the main conclusion that stands out in this analysis of advertisements compared in the *Which Ad Pulled Best?* examples. Whatever the example, the difference in the way people react to an advertisement can be traced back to the benefit: its believability, how important it was, and how compellingly it was presented to the people who read it.

It takes insight, of course, to determine the key benefits of a product. It may require systematic research or the more hazardous trial and error of years of experience to narrow the possible benefits down to the ones that are of the essence to a product's competitive advantage. Furthermore, it takes skill to transmit the benefit idea through all the media and techniques of mass communication, keeping it fresh over time.

When benefits are presented in the following ways, advertisements will, in general, produce better results.

1. Name the benefit. Be specific about it.

The more specific advertisements are the more successful ones. This holds true regardless of the type of publication, audience, or product. As an example, an advertisement headlined *Low-cost steam—Shop assembled and ready to use* pulled 100 percent more readership than *Steam That Satisfies.*

Similarly, of two advertisements illustrating the same foldaway table for stores, the advertisement headlined *Move up to $100 in iced watermelons in 8 sq. ft. of space* sold 3-1/2 times as much merchandise as the one headlined *8 square feet of dynamic display.*

An offer for a recipe book that included a detailed table of contents drew 136 percent more returns than the offer that merely announced 64 pages packed with methods, recipes, and tips on freezing and canning.

Of two advertisements run under the heading *Relax in Daks*, the one in which the body copy described these slacks most specifically with "No belt, no pressure around the middle. Hidden sponge rubber pads keep a polite but firm grip on your shirt" produced six times as many inquiries as the vaguer "They're self-supporting, shirt-controlling, and leave the body perfectly free."

For a self-sealing envelope, the U.S. Envelope Company tested eight different headlines. Some of the approaches were *So sanitary; Novel; Different; Better; Humid weather never affects.* However, by far, the most successful headline read *Avoid licking glue,* which was the most tangible, specific benefit.

The headline, though, doesn't work alone. *It's amazing! It's sensational! It's exclusive!* This received twice as much response as *How to become a popular dancer overnight.* Although the winning headline consisted of generalities, the advertisement itself contained a specific element that the other did not—a detailed diagram of one of the basic dance steps.

2. The product is the big benefit. Tell what it will do.

The more successful advertisements lay greater emphasis on the product. Greater product emphasis coincides with greater success. This is demonstrated by the advertisement headlined *How to get good pictures for sure.* In this advertisement was a large illustration of the camera. It received nearly twice as many inquiries as the one with the same headline that pictured an attractive man and woman gazing admiringly at the very small camera in their hands. In the first advertisement, the product was the hero and held center stage.

What is true of art emphasis is also true of headline-idea emphasis. *Amazing new low-priced electric sprayer for home use makes painting easy* sold 66 percent more sprayers than did the more humanly interesting *Now Tom does every home painting job himself.* This is because the first headline focuses on the product.

In another example, the catchy but not readily grasped headline *Cool heads in hot spots won't let you down* lost overwhelmingly to the straightforward *Copper's blue ribbon ventilators for workers' safety, health, comfort, efficiency.* Although this headline won't win any writing awards, it does focus unmistakably on the product.

Sometimes other factors may negate somewhat the effect of product emphasis. An example is that of two advertisements for the same manufacturer, one of which was headlined *Thatcher's 98 years of heating experience means greater comfort at lower cost.* A stark, cold feeling was conveyed by illustrations of four different pieces of heating equipment. The headline for the second advertisement was *Indoor weather made-to-order without lifting your finger.* Here were shown a man and woman in an attractively decorated room, along with a subordinate illustration that featured the one piece of heating equipment needed to provide this "indoor weather." This second advertisement, which pulled three times as many responses, is not only more specific and more humanly interesting, but it also gives more evidence of the benefit to be attained by actual use.

Another example of exceptions to emphasis on product is furnished by a pair of advertisements for Koppers BMU. One is a highly technical discussion of the structure and physical properties of the product. The other, more successful, advertisement, while containing the technical information, features a different approach: Under a photograph of a piece of soap, a man's shirt, and a plastic dish is the headline *Make them whiter and brighter with Koppers BMU.*

3. Make it easy for consumers to visualize the benefit. Keep your advertisements simple.

In one respect or another, simpler advertisements are consistently more successful. Example: For advertisers seeking direct replies, advertisements that include a coupon, thus making it easier for consumers to take action, receive a greater response than those without a coupon for reply.

In addition to looking at simplicity as being synonymous with ease, one can consider it an antonym of complexity. In this sense, those advertisements having a single rather than a multiple focus come out ahead. Eastman Kodak, for example, ran an advertisement divided into four sections. The main headline was *See what you can do with your present equipment.* Each of the four sections featured a different company product. Another issue of the same publication presented a Eastman Kodak advertisement headlined *Because photography is accurate to the last detail.* This was illustrated with a group of mechanical drawings. The copy story was "The magic of photography turns hours of costly drafting room time into a minute-quick job of utmost accuracy."

This second advertisement received 25 percent more attention and 125 percent more readership. Why should this be? The first advertisement was dramatic in its layout, but it made the reader decide on which section to direct his or her attention and on which story to concentrate. Although this multiple-interest advertisement attracted largely the same notice, it lagged far behind the readership earned by the advertisement that developed a single, simple story.

Similarly, an advertisement headlined *Great new insurance plan pays hospital, surgical expenses* did not offer as many benefits as the alternative version, *Now great new insurance plan offers you protection for hospital, surgical, and/or doctors' bills and/or lost income.* Yet the former, simpler advertisement pulled twice as many inquiries as the latter advertisement, indicating that it is sometimes a mistake to tell too much.

This principle still holds even in very small advertisements. A small, one-column advertisement illustrated with only a large bottle read *On our anniversary we're offering you Welch's Grape Juice at a new low price.* When, to this single theme, the company added a party flavor - children in the illustration wearing party hats and the headline *We are playing host to the nation on our anniversary with the greatest price reduction in Welch's history*—it lost readership.

Simplicity also results from unity of concept when a single theme is developed in headline, artwork, and copy. Two advertisements run for a perforator by Cummins Business Machines offer examples. One had a charming illustration of a young mother putting a cookie jar high on a shelf, out of the reach of her mischievous-looking, young son. The headline read *Mr. President—remove opportunity before—not after—fraud.* The second advertisement had no true illustration. On a bold background in white letters made of dots, as if done by a perforator, was the headline *You can't erase a hole. These tiny holes can save you from serious loss.*

In the first advertisement the analogy between the kind and thoughtful mother and the kind and thoughtful employers, each looking out for those dependent upon them, is not farfetched. But in the second and far more successful advertisement, no inferences, however apt, have to be drawn between separate concepts—the entire advertisement consists of one simple, clearly developed idea. Also, the language of the first advertisement is less specific—necessarily so, because a detailed discussion of cookie jars would bear little relation to the perforator being advertised. The point is, then, that not only the simplicity of any single concept, but also the relationship between the product and the consumer, makes the benefit evident.

4. Emphasize the benefit as much as possible. Use large space.

Small space advertisements can work very well. Talk to the average copywriter, however, and you'll soon find that he or she prefers to work with larger space units. In the larger space you can tell readers more about what the product can do for them. You can use a larger illustration to show more clearly what the product is and how it works. You can use more text material to tell why it is worth the purchase price. You can use larger type to make the copy easier to read and give the headline more impact. A more forceful overall impression can be made by increasing size alone.

Of a group of advertisements almost identical except for size, the larger ones will almost always do as well or better than the smaller versions. However, the cost per reader for inquiries or sales is often higher for large advertisements that use size only for size's sake.

Large space will not work wonders if the content of the advertisement is poor. Technique might also be a factor causing a smaller advertisement to outpull a larger one. "Technique," in this instance, may refer to such factors as stronger headlines, more clever themes, or more striking, attention-getting illustrations.

Evidence of the efficiency of smaller advertisements is provided in detail by the *Reader's Digest,* which naturally has an interest in convincing advertisers that their smaller advertisements can compete with bigger versions in magazines of conventional size. Although the *Digest* research is impressive, there are in many advertisers' minds distinct visual advantages to working in larger formats.

5. Don't obscure the benefit. The cute, the catchy, or the tricky may not work.

Being cute, catchy, or tricky is subordinate to conveying consumer benefits. Example: A transit card showing a squirrel saying *Take chances? Not me. I'm saving today* lost out to a more direct, more product-oriented card picturing a man saying *My bank—to 1,700,000 Canadians.*

Then, too, there was the lack of success of a comic strip treatment used by a maker of medical supplies such as adhesives, bandages, and back plasters. In tests against three different conventional advertisements, one of which was all type, the comic strip approach was a distant loser. Comic strip illustrations for advertisements about shaving and house painting also showed up badly. The lesson is that a technique associated predominantly with entertainment is often not suitable for selling certain types of products. An advertiser who is considering the use of such a technique may find it desirable to run some tests to see how appropriate it is for the product.

This does not mean that the catchy picture or phrase should summarily be rejected—on the contrary, reader-stopping headlines and tricky illustrations have been outstandingly successful. Without such advertising there would be a gray sameness to advertising as a whole. That's the reason there's room for the "different" approach used by the Franklin Institute. When they changed formats from a conventional approach to an offbeat one, the difference in results was striking. In the conventional display advertisement, the headline said *Work for Uncle Sam.* An advertisement that imitated a classified ad in which the small type was encircled far outshone the display ad. *Get on Uncle Sam's payroll* was given a bold, black line pointing to a coupon offering further information. This was an appropriate, simple way to sell a training course.

6. Get personal about the benefit, but don't get personal without a purpose.

It is generally accepted that formal, impersonal, and passive phraseology is undesirable for mass advertising. You are reminded constantly by copy experts to be—in most advertising—personal and informal. Still, being personal isn't always the key to interest and readership. For instance, an Eastman Kodak headline *Because photography is accurate to the last detail* was less personal but more successful than the one beginning *See what you can do with. . . .*

Once again, the advertiser should consider the individual circumstances, because the "be personal" advice can't always be applied. A writer of advertising to doctors or engineers will sensibly avoid too much familiarity in addressing such readers but will use "you" and "your" freely in writing trade advertising addressed to retailers.

Much depends upon whether the conversational feeling is appropriate for the advertising you're writing. If it is, then informality is desirable—certainly the case for much consumer print advertisements and all radio advertising.

Using "your" or "you" prominently doesn't necessarily guarantee anything. For example, 17 advertisements doing so were tested against 17 others that did not. Eight of the "you" advertisements were successful, but nine of the other ads were, too. No earth-shaking conclusions may be drawn here, but the figures back the point that the mere inclusion of personal words is no certain route to success.

7. The benefit is not always rational.

In addition to the tangible benefits from using the product, there may be intangible benefits. This is especially so for many products where the physical differences between it and its competitor are not that great. The taste of two colas may be preferred by similar proportions of the population, but the meaning that Pepsi and Coke have to their loyal users varies significantly. How an ad conveys and reinforces that meaning, through its words and visuals, can be as important as some product's tangible benefits.

What to Do to Get Attention, Create Desire, and Get Action When You Write Advertisements

For many years, advertising has been thought of as being part of a process that begins with creating **A**wareness, then strengthening the awareness to build **I**nterest, which then becomes **D**esire, which leads to **A**ction. This is often called the "AIDA" model of advertising effect. More recently, many alternative views of advertising's role have been offered. Today almost everyone recognizes that AIDA is a greatly oversimplified description of the process. Advertising effect is not necessarily linear, individual steps may be skipped entirely, and emotion-based response, which many feel lies outside the AIDA model, can be more important than the cognitive-based response. Despite this evolution, AIDA remains a useful way to think about advertising performance. Its different steps are relevant because all advertising should be successful on at least one of them. Important also is to understand that the individual components of an ad do not influence each of the AIDA dimensions equally. The aspects of an ad that may go toward building awareness are not necessarily the same ones that go in to building interest, desire, or action. So, in this context, we turn to AIDA to help us think about advertising effect.

In the AIDA model, attention and interest factors are closely related in advertising. First, you attract the attention of possible readers; then you invite them to read the message by switching quickly from mere eye catching to interest building. Most frequently, attention and interest are developed through headline and illustration treatment. After that, the first paragraph of copy is simply a transition from the ideas conveyed by the headline and illustration, to additional support for the message.

ATTENTION

In order to tell anyone about something, you first must get attention. This is true in personal conversation, mass communication, and advertising. Attention is meaningless, however, if it is not directed toward the product you're selling. Thus, it makes sense to properly draw the attention of the flip-and-run reader or the dial-turning television viewer to your message.

Advertisements that draw reader attention directly to a product benefit capture that interest more solidly than those that use attention-getting techniques merely for the sake of getting interest per se. Accordingly, a headline is more likely to attract attention if it promises a shortcut to a housewife scanning the shopping news. In a business publication, an illustration that visibly portrays a manufacturing cost cutter will be more likely to attract the attention of management-minded readers.

Importance of Attention Getting Varies with Audiences

Although attention getting has an effect on advertising results in all media, it is more important in some media than in others, especially in situations where you don't have a captive audience.

Consider a highly rated television show that holds you captive up to the moment the commercial flashes on the screen. Your attention is more assured than in the magazine where the nature of the consumption process is to move on to the next page. In both cases, though, it may vanish quickly if the message doesn't offer an immediate promise of reward. Attention getting is more important to the television advertiser who uses a station break following the final commercial of a preceding program or whose advertising appears in an extended pod of other commercials. Such an advertiser cannot rely on the same degree of captivity as the final one above.

Magazine and newspaper advertisers have a great problem in capturing reader attention. Because there is nothing of the captive audience here, such advertisers fight for attention, especially when they face competing advertisements on the same or adjoining pages.

Physical Elements Play a Part

Size, color, and unusual treatments attract attention, but a mere increase in size, the addition of color, or a switch to more unusual illustrations may not be enough. These techniques are successful in attracting attention only if they make the promise of a benefit more apparent to the audience. For example, we know from research that a dominant element such as a big illustration will increase attention. Still, to make this increased attention meaningful, the illustration should be relevant to the product and/or interests of readers.

Inevitably, we return to the principle that the content of communication is more vital to successful rapport with readers, viewers, and listeners than are the mechanical means of expression. It is what you say and show that provides the key to attention—the ideas, the suggestions of value, the promise of benefits to be received. Headlines and illustrations are simply tools for projecting that value.

INTEREST

Attracting interest in your advertising depends on both the tangible aspects, such as physical attributes, and the intangible ones, such as appealing ideas.

The advertisements whose physical attributes do the best job of translating attention into interest are the ones that are mechanically the easiest to read. Such advertisements are organized so logically that information is easy for the reader to grasp. Picture-caption advertisements illustrate the point, as do those set in easy-to-read typefaces and those from which all distracting elements have been cut.

Still, the value of a physically perfect advertisement will be small if the ideas are mundane. It is the ideas conveyed by the first elements of an advertisement that either build or preclude sufficient interest for the reader to want to dig deeper into the message.

You will find some advertisements that clearly demonstrate to the reader the benefit of finding out what's good about the products and how they will fit his or her needs. These advertisements are high in general interest, promise a story, suggest an answer to a universal problem, touch the reader's self-interest, look as if they contain specific information of great interest, and contain believable illustrations of the product in action.

DESIRE

More than anything else, the purpose of an advertisement is to create a desire to own the product or use the service being advertised. As you will see from the researched advertisements in this book, most of the highly rated ones start immediately to build desire into headlines, illustrations, and introductory copy. Once again the importance of headline and illustration becomes apparent. One respected advertising agency head, in fact, told his creative people, "Put *everything* in the headline." To him, the reason for placing copy under a headline is to make the headline more important, rather than draw attention to, or get results from, the copy itself. Few will agree that copy is *that* unimportant, arguing that it reinforces the ideas offered in the headlines and illustration. Copy, they say, reassures readers in many, and often new, ways that the product will benefit them to the point of convincing them to think about it in a more favorable way than they had before.

Results accrue from a composite of the effects created by headlines, illustrations, and copy. Yet the key almost always lies in the first impression conveyed in headlines and illustrations. If you can determine which advertisement the readers feel offers the greatest benefit, you will have found the one that achieves the most results.

Specific, relevant, unique, believable, and wanted benefits are the touchstones of desire creation in successful advertising.

ACTION

Although immediate action is usually not expected from an advertisement, ultimate action and/or beliefs is always anticipated or hoped for. Because action is especially sought in mail order, or direct response, advertising, let us consider action in these terms.

In addition to direct sales, one measurement of effectiveness is the number of inquiries received. Inquiries come from people who presumably are good prospects. One way to spur inquiries is to use a coupon. Although couponed advertisements will generally outpull couponless ones, this is not always true—a couponless advertisement may have offered a benefit more relevant to the kind of people who were logical prospects for what was offered in the coupon.

You will also find instances in which smaller advertisements produced more inquiries than larger ones, and some cases in which larger advertisements were better at spurring action. A seeming contradiction? Not if you recognize that the mechanics of space size are not so important as the mental impact delivered by the idea quality of the content.

Moral: If you can use a larger space to create a picture of greater benefits, use it; but if you can't, use smaller advertisements with the possible added benefit of increasing reach or frequency. As the Newspaper Advertising Bureau has pointed out over and over again in its studies of copy effectiveness in newspapers, it's content that counts.

Another action question relating to mail order: Will inquiry returns drop if you charge for the sample or booklet offered? This question comes up when an advertiser offers something of value in general media. Such an advertiser usually wants to limit inquiries to logical prospects. Putting a nominal price on the offer is one way to make sure that inquiries will come from prospects only. Still, an advertiser hesitates to impose any block (even a small price) in the way of customer action.

In general, the results seem to vary more with what is offered than with the price of action. A charge for a worthwhile offer does not seem to reduce inquiries. Furthermore, in many cases of free offers, advertisers stress that there is no charge but neglect to put proper emphasis on the offer itself. It sometimes seems advis-

able to stress the value of the offer and play down the price or the fact that the offer is free.

All advertising is designed to produce sales in the long run, and only a small portion is aimed at direct orders obtained through advertising. As a rule, the copy researcher does not have actual sale results with which to demonstrate the effectiveness of advertisements. They are most often looking at whether dispositions to use the product have been increased or attitudes about the brand have been enhanced. In mail order, the researcher has a solid measure of success—the number of orders obtained. This puts mail order in a class apart from other advertising.

SUMMARY

The most important element in producing sales results is the benefit to the customer described in advertising. It is the strong benefit that leads to more attention, interest, desire, and ultimately, action. Gimmicks, gadgets, and other techniques are distinctly subordinate to strong benefits.

Note that the mail order advertiser who piles benefit upon benefit, makes the value to the consumer most evident, unique, and believable, and makes such value and benefit the most easily obtainable is the one who wins out.

PACT Principles of Copy Testing

In 1982, twenty-one of the major U.S. advertising agencies issued a public statement called PACT (Positioning Advertising Copy Testing). PACT represented their consensus on the fundamental principles underlying a good copy testing system. Although many of these agencies have now merged, some with their names and identities lost, the principles still provide a solid foundation for understanding the use of effective advertising research.

The following advertising agencies sponsored PACT: N.W. Ayer, Inc.; Ted Bates Worldwide, Inc.; Batten, Barton, Durstine & Osborne, Inc.; Benton & Bowles, Inc.; Campbell-Mithun, Inc.; Dancer Fitzgerald Sample, Inc.; D'Arcy-MacManus & Masius, Inc.; Doyle Dane Bernbach, Inc.; Grey Advertising, Inc.; Kenyon & Eckhardt, Inc.; KM&G International, Inc.; Marschalk Campbell-Ewald Worldwide; Marsteller, Inc.; McCaffrey and McCall Inc.; McCann-Erickson, Inc.; Needham, Harper & Steers, Inc. Ogilvy & Mather, Inc.; SSC&B: Lintas Worldwide; J. Walter Thompson Company; Young & Rubicam.

Principle 1:
A good copy testing system provides measurements that are relevant to the objectives of the advertising.

Advertising is used (as are all marketing tools) to contribute to the achievement of marketing objectives—whether they be for a product, a service, or a corporation. The industry recognizes (as exemplified by the landmark "DAGMAR" [1] study of the ANA) that the goal of advertising is to achieve specified objectives. It is further recognized that different advertisements can have a number of objectives, such as the following:

- Reinforcing current perceptions.
- Encouraging trial of a product or service.
- Encouraging new uses of a product or service.
- Providing greater saliency for a brand or company name.
- Changing perceptions and imagery.
- Announcing new features and benefits.

To be useful, a copy test for a given advertisement should be designed to provide an assessment of the advertisement's potential for achieving its stated objectives. Indeed, advertising objectives should be the first issue for discussion when a copy testing program is to be developed or a particular method is to be selected. In recognition of the fundamental importance of these objectives, every copy testing proposal and every report on results should begin with a clear statement of the advertising objectives.

Principle 2:
A good copy testing system is one which requires agreement about how the results will be used in advance of each specific test.

A primary purpose of copy testing is to *help* in deciding whether or not to run the advertising in the marketplace. A useful approach is to specify what are called "action standards" before the results are in. The following are some examples of possible action standards.

- Significantly improve perceptions of the brand as measured by _____.
- Achieve an attention level of no longer than _____ percent as measured by _____.

---

[1] "Defining Advertising Goal for Measured Advertising Results," by the Association of National Advertisers, Copyright 1961.

- Perform at least as well as (specify execution) as measured by _____.

- Produce negative responses of no higher than _____ percent as measured by _____.

The practice of specifying how the results will be used before they are in ensures that there is mutual understanding on the goals of the test and minimizes conflicting interpretations of the test once the results are in.

Moreover, prior discussion allows for the proper positioning of the action standards, because the copy test results are not, in most cases, the sole information used in deciding whether to use a particular advertisement. The results of any given copy test should be viewed in the context of a body of learning. Thus, prior discussion should take into account the following:

- How well the particular copy testing method used relates to the objectives of the advertising.

- The *range* of results that are realistically achievable for the advertising approach used and for the brand or company in question.

- The entire search context (including other types of studies) for the tested ad and for similar ads.

A discussion of these issues prior to initiating a copy test provides benefits for both the advertisers and the agency. It minimizes the risks inherent in using copy test results in a mechanistic way, isolated from other learning. It maximizes the opportunity to draw upon learning and seasoned judgment of the advertiser and the agency as both parties reach for the best possible advertising.

Principle 3:
A good copy testing system provides *multiple* measurements, because single measurements are generally inadequate to assess the performance of an advertisement.

With the exception of corporate advocacy advertising, it is commonly believed that the ultimate measurement by which advertising should be judged is its *contribution* to sales. But the complexity of the marketing process and the constraints of time and money usually preclude rigorous testing—that is, testing which can separate the effects of advertising from the many other factors that influence sales and thereby provide an estimate of the sales contribution of a given advertisement prior to a national launch. There is also no universally accepted single measurement which can serve as a surrogate for sales.

Moreover, the communication process is complex. To understand this process, and to learn from each successive test, it is necessary to use multiple measures—measures that reflect the multifaceted nature of communications. However, the inclusion of multiple measures should not imply that all measures have equal weight in evaluating the advertising. As noted previously, in advance of each test, agreement should be reached as to the relative importance of the various measurements in judging the acceptability of the tested execution.

Principle 4:
A good copy testing system is based on a model of human response to communications—the *reception* of a stimulus, the comprehension of the stimulus, and the *response* to the stimulus.

PACT agencies view advertising as performing on several levels. To succeed, an advertisement must have an effect:

- On the "eye," on the "ear": *It must be received* (RECEPTION).

- On the "mind": *It must be understood* (COMPREHENSION).

- On the "heart": *It must make an impression* (RESPONSE).

It therefore follows that a good copy testing system should answer a number of questions. Listed below are examples of the kinds of questions relevant to these communications issues. The order of the listing does not relate to priority of importance. As discussed in the preceding principles, priorities will vary depending on the objectives of the specific advertising being tested.

Reception
— Did the advertising "get through"?
— Did it catch the consumer's attention?
— Was it remembered?
— Did it catch his or her eye? His or her ear?

Comprehension
— Was the advertising understood?
— Did the consumer "get" the message?
— Was the message identified with the brand?
— Was anything confusing or unclear?

Response

— Did the consumer accept the proposition?

— Did the advertising affect attitudes toward the brand?

— Did the consumer think or "feel" differently about the brand after exposure?

— Did the advertising affect perceptions of the brand?

— Did the advertising alter perceptions of the set of competing brands?

— Did the consumer respond to direct action appeals?

Another area of response measurements relates to executional elements. PACT agencies agree that it is useful to obtain responses to these elements of an advertisement.

Executional diagnostics: Questioning about consumers' reactions to the advertising execution (e.g., perceived differentiation from other advertising, reactions to music, to key phrases, to presenters or characters, to story elements, etc.) can provide insight about the strengths and weaknesses of the advertising and why it performed as it did.

PACT agencies use different measures to address the issues in these four areas. However, they are all based on the same fundamental understanding of the communication process.

Principle 5:
A good copy testing system allows for consideration of whether the advertising stimulus should be exposed more than once.

Extensive experimentation in the field of communications and learning has demonstrated that learning of test material is far higher after two exposures than after one—and that subsequent exposures do not yield as large an increase as that between the first and second exposure.

In light of the experimental work, PACT agencies share the view that the issue of single versus multiple exposures should be carefully considered in each test situation. There are situations in which a single exposure would be sufficient—given the objectives of the advertising and the nature of the test methodology. There are other situations where a single exposure could be inadequate—particularly high-risk situations,

subtle or complex communications, or questioning about executional diagnostics.

Principle 6:
A good copy testing system recognizes that the more finished a piece of copy is, the more soundly it can be evaluated and requires, as a minimum, that alternative executions be tested to the same degree of finish.

Experience has shown that test results can often vary depending on the degree of finish of the test executions. Thus, careful judgment should be used in considering the importance of what may be lost in a less-than-finished version. Sometimes this loss may be consequential; sometimes it may be critical.

The judgment of the advertising creators should be given great weight as to the degree of finish required to represent the finished advertisement for test purposes. If there is a reason to believe that alternative executions would be unequally penalized in the preproduction form, then it is generally advisable to test them in a more finished form. If alternative executions are tested in different stages of finish within the same test, then it is impossible to ensure that the results are not biased because of the varying degrees of finish.

Principle 7:
A good copy testing system provides controls to avoid the biasing effects of exposure context.

Extensive work in the field of communications and learning has demonstrated that the perception of and response to a stimulus is affected by the context in which the stimulus is presented and received.

In the case of advertising, it has been demonstrated, for example, that recall of the same commercial can vary depending on a number of conditions—such as whether exposure to the commercial:

- Is off-air versus on-air.
- Is in a cluttered reel of commercials versus a program context.
- Is in one specific program context versus another specific program context.

Thus, PACT agencies share the view that it is imperative to control the biasing effects of variable exposure contexts.

Principle 8:
A good copy testing system is one that takes into account basic considerations of sample definition.

- The testing should be conducted among a sample of the target audience for the advertised product. Limiting testing to the general population without provision for separate analysis of the target audience can be misleading.

- The sample should be representative of the target audience. To the degree that the sample drawn does not represent the target audience, the users of the research should be informed about the possible effects of the lack of representativeness on the interpretation of test results.

- The sample should take into account any geographic differences if they are critical to the assessment of the performance of a brand or service.

- The sample should be of sufficient size to allow a decision based on the obtained data to be made with confidence.

Principle 9:

A good copy testing system is one that can demonstrate reliability and validity.

To provide results that can be used with confidence, a copy testing system should be:

- *Reliable.* It should yield the same results each time the advertising is tested. If, for example, a test of multiple executions does not yield the same rank order of performance on the test/retest, the test is not reliable and should not be used to judge the performance of commercials. Tests in which external variables are not held constant will probably yield unreliable results.

- *Valid.* It should provide results that are relevant to marketplace performance. PACT agencies recognize that demonstration of validity is a major and costly undertaking requiring industry wide participation. Although some evidence of predictive validity is available, many systems are in use for which no evidence of validity is provided. We encourage the cooperation of advertisers and agencies in pursuit of this critical need.

Interviews with Experts: Answers to Common and Important Questions about Advertising

This section presents interviews with some leading advertising authorities. They discuss candidly and informally various aspects of print advertising, with special emphasis on creative matters.

Also included is an interview with the late George Gallup, which has appeared in each of the previous editions of *Which Ad Pulled Best?* It is repeated largely as it was originally given, although some dated material has been deleted. Because it provides valuable insights by one of the great authorities in communication, it has been included again. Furthermore, the principles expressed by Dr. Gallup are timeless in their application.

In some instances the questions asked of the experts are similar. It is interesting and valuable to see how different respondents answer the same questions and—in so many instances—to see how closely they agree on the basic principles of advertising and advertising creativity.

George Gallup
GALLUP & ROBINSON, INC.

Q: In the course of the years, have you found much change in the way advertising works—in the kind of advertising that works best?

A: No, I wouldn't say so. The copywriters change. But the kind of copy that has always worked still works. The problem is not so much one of finding out what new appeals work better today as it is of educating the new people who are coming along all the time in the basic principles of advertising. And, as a matter of fact, the old-timers seem to need reminding every now and then on the basics. We have to keep reproving old truths in terms of new products and new markets.

Q: In the course of your experience with advertisers—and particularly with their advertising agencies—has any particular weak spot in the whole process of presenting sales ideas in advertising struck you as most needing correction?

A: Well, I suppose there are a lot of weak spots. I'd say that the most greatly overlooked opportunity is that of advertising products. We find an awful lot of advertisers seem to be afraid to tell people about their products. But the public is very interested in products. They want to know all about these products that they can buy.

We have too much advertising that starts out talking about something else that is presumably of great interest to prospective customers and then, after an involved transition, gets around to admitting that something's for sale. Actually, people read ads because they want to know what's for sale.

Q: You say that people want to know about prices and about what's new in products and about what products will do. Would you say that any one of these elements is most important?

A: No, because it depends on the product, on competition in the field, and on the different levels of different kinds of merchandise—and on a lot of other things. But I would say that there's an awful lot more news about products than many advertisers recognize. The opportunity is there for copy people to search out newsy things about products. A new price is in itself news. A new product is news. A new ingredient is news. A way of making a product stronger is news. There are a million and one things about products that relate to the benefits to be secured from buying them that are news. It's up to the copy people to wring this information out of the production people who know the facts but who don't realize their (the facts') value to advertising.

Q: Is it the words, then, that are used in advertising copy that make the difference? Does the phraseology?

A: No, not words or phrases, but *ideas.* That's what distinguishes, perhaps more than anything else, the advertising that penetrates from that which does not get under the skin of the people who see or read or hear it. The important thing is to present ideas forcefully. Words and images are the vehicles, of course, for all expression. But they are not good unless they mean something worthwhile to the folks on the receiving end.

Q: Could you be a little more specific in what you mean by the forceful presentation of ideas?

A: This big difference between advertisements—it's not one of using magic words. Boast copy is no good, no matter how many so–called magic words are strewn all the way through it. Proof copy, on the other hand—that is, believable proof copy—is the kind of thing that sticks with people. Demonstrations always have been effective. The before-and-afters are magic, not because of the words used or the size of the pictures so much as because of the magic in the idea, the proof of value.

One of the most interesting things about this whole question is that the kind of advertising that is most effective is the kind that is approved by the general public. The advertisements that cause complaints by the public are those that miss the boat—the boastful advertisements, the ones with the lack of proof, the ones that are cluttered up with "adiness" rather than performing the service for which advertising is ideally suited: telling people about the true benefits of merchandise.

Q: How about the physical appearance of advertisements? Is there any general criterion that separates the good from the bad advertising in this respect?

A: I guess the most generally applicable rule of thumb would be to separate advertisements into those with gimmicks and those without. The gimmicky advertisements usually don't work. Gimmicks tend to get in the way of idea expression. By this I mean all kinds of gimmicks: trick headlines, color just for the sake of

adding something extra, unusual typography, excessive use of tint block, copy patches that mutilate a main illustration, crazy pictures that have no relation to the product being sold. These things create "adiness"; they take away from the clear expression of the many things about products that are of very great interest to the public.

Q: Along these lines, it seems as though quite a lot of advertisers believe that they have to entertain as they sell. Aren't many of these gimmicks put in for entertainment value of a sort?

A: I suppose many of the gimmicks are put in for entertainment value. But the thing is that people don't read advertisements to be entertained so much as to learn something about the products. It all comes back to the lack of appreciation of the interest of the public in merchandise—not just plain old merchandise, but new merchandise, new things about merchandise, new ways to use merchandise. There's plenty of entertainment value of a sort in the products, provided the copy writer is smart enough to find it and present it in a forthright and interesting manner.

Q: Do you find that in a medium such as TV (technologically so far removed from, say, magazine advertising) the kind of copy approach that is most effective is very different from those that you have found resultful in other media?

A: No, not really. In television there is a difference that results from having a captive audience to start with. You can jump right into the selling copy without having to snag attention first. The attention is there, so you go directly into the interest- and desire-building process. Tricky wind-ups and abstruse lead-ins are usually a waste of valuable time in TV commercials. Additionally, in television you have the added dimensions of sound and motion to help. But aside from these considerations, the basics of persuasion are the same.

Q: How long has Gallup & Robinson been testing TV commercials?

A: We have been operating a television service—serving regular clients in this respect—since November of 1951. For about two years before that time, we were developing the research methods we use.

Q: *Could you describe in very general terms what those methods are?*

A: Very briefly, our methods of judging TV impact are of the same nature as those we apply in studying the impact of magazine advertisements. We concern ourselves with the thoughts and feelings a person has when an advertiser tries to register his sales message with him or her. We are looking at how well the advertising succeeds in making an impression and doing it in a persuasive fashion.

Q: *Do you find much difference in the impact made by different TV commercials?*

A: Oh, yes—a tremendous amount of difference. On average we experience a more than six-to-one difference in the levels of recall and persuasion. And then, of course, we get wide range in the playback of the selling messages and in the conviction, believability, and involvement that become apparent. You've got to keep in mind that the advertiser is paying the same amount of money to reach each of these levels of effectiveness.

Q: *How did the G&R Impact methodology evolve?*

A: At Young & Rubicam, we gained important insights about the methodology itself. While readership findings proved to be extremely helpful in reaching a larger audience with the advertiser's message, they did not provide all the information that was needed to produce effective advertising. The findings did not, for example, reveal how many of those who had seen or read given advertisements registered on the copy message or, for that matter, on the brand name. Nor did they shed light on the buying urge created by the copy.

To bridge this gap, a series of experiments was undertaken during the late 1930s and the early 1940s. This experimentation resulted in the development of the Impact method, which sought to move beyond reading and noting data and to measure such factors as registration of brand name and such qualitative parameters as idea communication and urge to buy. The new method could be used not only with print but with broadcast advertising as well. The first test of the method was a stripped-down copy of the April 16, 1945, issue of *Life* magazine with test ads "tipped-in." While we were working on these experiments at Young & Rubicam between 1945 and 1947, Dr.

Claude Robinson, who founded Opinion Research Corporation (ORC), was conducting similar studies with a magazine called *Space.*

This experimentation eventually lead to the Impact method, which was fully in place by 1945. In 1947 I left Y&R to join Claude Robinson in a new venture called Gallup & Robinson to carry on research in advertising.

Q: *As you look back over your career in research, would you give us your impression of the various trends or changes that have occurred?*

A: There have been many, many schools, one succeeding the other, in the history of copy research, when everybody ran this way and then ran that way. Of course, this is true in every field; one school succeeds another. But I think there's a trend back to the basics—not only in the United States, but all around the world. The first job of advertising is to get seen and read and then to change people's attitudes toward it.

Q: *How would that translate itself in terms of either research techniques or research philosophies?*

A: I don't think it would change the philosophies. The techniques need to be redefined and improved. This whole problem of isolating and weighing the influence of advertising on a sale is a very sticky problem and always has been. You're trying to isolate advertising and its influence; you're trying to sort it out from a hundred other identifiable factors. I think it can be done, and it's amazing to me that more people aren't studying from year to year the advertising that is succeeding and what the factors are that are common to it as opposed to the advertising which demonstrably isn't succeeding.

Q: *How should an advertiser evaluate how effective his or her advertising is?*

A: Almost every campaign, to begin with, has specific objectives. The whole process of advertising is designing a strategy that will create a sale. You can find out if the strategy is working. Are you changing people's minds about this particular fact about the product? You can measure that. Every advertiser, even if he spends only a few thousand dollars, should demand some kind of evidence of the effectiveness of his advertising. And I am shocked, really, that sometimes advertisers spend millions of dollars without demanding that kind of evidence.

Q: Of course, there are various schools of copy testing.

A: And every school claims to be "the" school. But I think that the most useful, truthful way of thinking of copy testing is to regard all of the methods as useful and serving a given purpose. There isn't any method that will cover the waterfront. This is the mistake all schools of thought make. They believe if they find a cure for headache it will also cure flat feet; but one must know the limitations of each method. Being a good copy researcher is a matter of knowing exactly what each method will do, what its strengths are, and what its limitations are and not trying to come to some overall conclusion that if it's good in this area it has to be great.

Q: What would you say is the major issue in survey research.

A: Sampling obviously has to be number one. In the first part of this century, it was bad sampling that made the *Literary Digest* come up with the most inaccurate poll results in history, an error of 19 percentage points on a presidential election. They were sampling by mail and sampling people who had telephones and automobiles, which at that time was relatively atypical. We changed that to quota sampling up to 1948. Then our mistake, our election of Tom Dewey instead of Truman in 1948, was due largely to timing factors. At that point in history, we had to stop about 10 days to 2 weeks before the election. After 1948 we had to invent ways of polling up through Saturday noon before election, because there are significant changes in those last few days. Now we can be accurate to tenths of percentage points.

Ted Bell
FORMER CHIEF CREATIVE OFFICER AT YOUNG & RUBICAM AND LEO BURNETT

Q: Let's start with establishing a definition of advertising—what you think it is, and what does it do?

A: Some people have called it the engine of capitalism. Advertising creates awareness of products and business services. Without advertising, nobody would know that there were six kinds of cars to buy, or toothpaste or soap. So advertising is the spreading of information; it's communicating news about products and also creating emotions about products in the marketplace.

Q: What role does advertising play in the buying process?

A: It creates demand and disseminates information.

Q: Let's turn the question around a little bit. Why do people look at advertising?

A: Well, first, advertising is ubiquitous. It's everything—television, print, newspapers. You can't shut it out. But the reason it is so present is that people crave information. They want to know about what they can buy. They are inquisitive. It's a part of human nature to want to know what's out there.

Q: Are there differences between print advertising and television advertising, or are they really the same things just in different forms?

A: I think they're closely related. A good ad, regardless of the media, presents an idea in a fresh way so that somebody will do something or think about a product or service in a different way. And for me, the best advertising ideas have a directness and simplicity to them. That's why print is such a good medium to work in. With print you have only the idea, a pen or pencil, and piece of paper. Too often what happens in broadcast and television is production and music and surface imagery take the place of an idea. You can't get away with that in print. The best advertising ideas have to be able to be done in print, or they may not be good ideas.

Q: Are there certain types of ideas that are easier or better to convey in print versus TV?

A: Yes and no. There are some things we wouldn't really want to do a commercial for. In the case of something that is highly technical, where there's a lot of technical writing or information that needs to be conveyed, we wouldn't want to be in a 30-second commercial. More likely, the idea can come alive in both media. There's a famous Volkswagen print ad from the old agency Doyle Dane Bernbach where I started. It showed the lunar landing module descending to the moon with a headline text saying, "It's ugly, but it gets you there," together with the Volkswagen logo.

Although the ad was not made into a TV commercial, you can imagine that it would make an equally great commercial. You would see the surface of the moon and all of a sudden, this little thing comes down into the frame and starts to get lower, lower, lower—you hear the sound effects, and you see this funny-looking thing, and it sits and settles on the surface of the moon and the dust flies up, and a little super comes up and says, "It's ugly but it gets you there." That is a great television commercial. The idea is the star, so it works in both media.

Q: If you're a U.S. company, why do you do print advertising?

A: Well, a lot of small companies do print because it's what they can afford. If you're a larger company and can afford both, I always recommend they do both. Let's say you're an automobile company. A 30-second commercial could be used to show beautiful running shots of a car so you see how beautiful the car is. A print ad could give you more information about the car to justify the $30,000 investment. You're not gonna just say "That's a pretty car. I'll go buy it." So that's one way print and TV work together.

Q: How does the audience to which the ad is directed fit into the process of creating the advertising?

A: You try to have this image of the market in your mind. Really good creative people have very good instincts about how most people think, how people will react to a given theme. It's hard to describe, but if I come up with an idea, I don't know how I know this, but I just know it will work. You have a feel for whether people will think it's funny, whether they'll understand it, and whether they'll like it. You have to have a sense of human nature and enormous common sense. I think the skills necessary for a creative person are intelligence, taste, and imagination. If you've got those, you'll be a pretty good advertising person.

Q: When you're thinking about an ad, how does the process evolve?

A: I start writing for myself as a member of my audience. If I don't think an idea's funny or fresh, I'm not gonna show it to anybody else. I put myself in the position of someone sitting at home by myself reading a magazine. Would I think the ad was funny, would I like it or believe it or hate it? Just write for your audience.

If you're writing a financial ad that's going to run in *Fortune,* you're going to write a different ad than if you're trying to sell soap to a woman in Des Moines who's interested in getting her son's boxer shorts clean. One of the first things you get in an advertising strategy is the target. For example, say kids 18–24. Okay, now you've helped me to start to figure out how I'm gonna think about this. I'm probably not going to do something cerebral; I'll probably do something with energy and fun. You think about the target. It puts you right into it.

Q: Can you take us through the process that you go through to develop a piece of print advertising?

A: Usually it begins with the client. They brief you on the problem—whether it's the lack of awareness for the product, a lack of differentiation for it, or low esteem. Then you go back and say, "All right, how are we gonna fix this? What's the solution to this problem?" And, typically, you create a strategy. You target the audience, say, men ages 20 to 30, upper income, some college. Then you develop a strategy, say, to convince the target these glass apples are the best glass apples in the world. You dig into the product to see why it's better, and then you come up with a strategic proposition. You may not explicitly see this in the advertising, but it's the foundation upon which the advertising is built that says what people need to hear about this product in order to want it. There are support points for it—the glass apple—Old World craftsmen, pure lead, etc. Then you go back to the client and you say, "Here's the strategy. We think we should talk about the apple's pure lead crystal and Old World craftsmanship." It's important for people to agree to the strategy up front so you don't have to spin your wheels. The strategy is given to the creative people to come up with an interesting way to talk about pure lead crystal and Old World craftsmanship.

Q: One often hears about rational advertising versus emotional advertising, or feature/benefit versus image. How relevant are these type of distinctions? Are they important, and if they are, what do they mean in terms of the type of advertising that you try to create?

A: They're all relevant, and they're all linked, and it depends on the product and category. You wouldn't want to be real rational about soft drink advertising. You know, you wouldn't want to explain to me why 7UP is a great product in rational terms. You could do that and it would be funny, but then it's emotional advertising. All advertising is emotional in some way because you have an emotional response to it no matter what. Even when you feel that advertising is very rational, you are having an emotional response. You can't not have an emotion, whether it's I hate it, I love it, or I'm bored. But the key is to figure out what you want to say to people and then say it in a way that makes them like you. If people like you they're much more willing to listen to what you're saying. And even if they don't quite believe it, they'll still pick you over the other guy because they like you. Think about McDonald's. They didn't get to be the largest hamburger chain by telling people what was in the hamburger. They got there because they made people love McDonald's, and all McDonald's advertising is designed to reinforce that. That's not to say that you don't need to promote, but, basically, their mission is to make people like McDonald's more than the other guy.

Q: How do you judge whether a print ad is effective? Do you look at the whole or do you look at the pieces?

A: The first thing I ask myself is, "Will I stop and look at this ad if I were reading the magazine?" If I'm reading the magazine and won't even look at it, then I don't even care what the ad says, because nobody's gonna pay attention to it. So the first question is, "Will it stop me?" Once I get past that point I say, "Is it compelling? Is it interesting? Is it funny? Does it tell me something I don't know? Does it have an idea, or is it just a headline and a picture? Is it artfully done? Is it intelligently written?" The great Bill Bernbach had a theory, and I think he's right. He believed advertising was part of the culture, and it's incumbent upon advertising agencies not to litter up the highways and byways of everybody's mind and physical space with junk. That underscores the place for intelligence and taste in advertising.

Q: How do you know when a piece of advertising becomes stale or needs to change?

A: You just seem to know, but there's a danger that you're so close to it that you and the client get tired of it before the public, which doesn't see it as much as you do.

Q: Some people think that the advertising environment is becoming more cluttered and people are being bombarded by all sorts of different approaches. What

implications does this have for the advertising messages that you create?

A: There was a time in the not too distant past where the whole country sat down and watched the *Ed Sullivan Show* all the way through. To sell something you could go on the *Ed Sullivan Show* and count on everybody seeing your message. That doesn't even come close to happening anymore. It's totally fractured, and there's far more advertising than ever before. You've got to stand out. You gotta stand up and be counted and get somebody to know you. Too much of today's advertising is safe and conservative, and that contributes to many messages not getting noticed. It's why you have to "break through" first.

Q: I've wondered if this more cluttered environment has implications for the relative importance of the individual executions versus the campaign itself. For large brands especially, like AT&T, you pay less attention to each individual ad, but together as a whole, all of the execution create a presence.

A: Individual or cumulative. Both are important. People form their opinions not based on any one execution but on the totality of the messages you're sending to them. I've had clients tell me, "You don't understand. We don't do image advertising." I disagree. Every ad you do is an image ad, because every time you run any commercial, people are going to have an image of you. So if you're doing clunky, boring advertising, you're a clunky, boring brand. You know, they're going to form an image of you based on what you tell them—what you send out there. You have a vision of Nike based on a lot of different sensory input that you had over the years from their advertising.

Q: Is there any one myth of advertising that you'd like to dispel?

A: Yes, that it's easy; it's really hard. It's easy to do sloppily. It's easy to do in an ordinary fashion. But it's hard to do something really good.

Q: For someone who is starting out now and thinking of getting into the creative side of the advertising business, what skills would you like to see them have?

A: You have to be a keen observer of human nature. You have to have a lot of common sense. You have to have a sense of humor and can't take yourself too seriously, and I think you've gotta have creative talent, which you can't go out and get at the store. Really good art directors are usually great copywriters, and terrific copywriters usually have a lot of taste and know what something should look like—what Leo Burnett called the "fitness of things." Although they're two discreet skills, when you are really talented in either one, you usually are pretty good in the other. Funny, isn't it?

Roy Grace
CREATIVE HALL OF FAME INDUCTEE

Q: What does successful advertising do?

A: There are several different levels on which you can answer this question. You could say advertising motivates the consumer to purchase your product. But that's an easy answer and an obvious one.

To truly answer the question, you have to get into that whole mysterious area of what comprises advertising and what motivates people. What's important here is that you have the reader or viewer participate in your advertising. We want people to get involved in the advertising, we want them to think, we want to do things that are provocative, that force them to wrap their minds around our proposition. All successful advertising does that. Unfortunately, the vast majority of advertising gathers no response whatsoever. People just don't see it, they don't hear it, because it doesn't recognize that essential issue which is: You must get somebody involved, you must make them think or feel.

Q: Could you position the role of advertising in the broader business context of the buying decision?

A: Advertising, in its simplest terms, provides information. It tells me that there's a sale going on, it tells me that your product has front-wheel drive and fuel injection. It provides information to the consumer. So it is a voice for the product, a voice for the manufacturer. It is their way of communicating and telling the public what ingredients they have in their product, what the benefits of their product are. What it really replaces is the salesman in the store, or the store window, to a certain degree. It imparts information to the consumer.

Where advertising gets again more complex is in the real world, where most products exist on a parity level with their competition. What's the difference between Drink "A" and Drink "B"? There is no differ-ence, and what advertising can do is create a difference. Advertising helps sell a product that may be on a parity with its competition. If the manufacturer is astute at choosing a good agency, he has bought himself a very forceful ally in selling his merchandise.

Advertising also helps improve products. When I improve a product, I use advertising to get out there as fast as I can to tell the world that I now have a new ingredient that gets your clothes whiter than they should dare be. This also alerts the competition that they've got to make a better product.

Q: How is television advertising different from print advertising, and how are they the same?

A: Television is an easier form to work in from a creative point of view. For one thing, your mistakes are easier to cover because of the medium's pace. You have an enormous asset that you don't have in print, and that's sound and music. You have the element of time, which works very much in your favor, so you can build dramatically. If you have to compare a 30-second commercial today with a printed page, in television you have 30 seconds to tell your message, while in print you have maybe a second and a half with a vague possibility that somebody will read the copy.

Print is a more difficult and rigorous discipline, and a lot of people can't do both. It's really interesting—some people can do television and have no concept of print, and some people can do print and have no concept of television. It's not that unusual to find that the reasons have to do with the person as an individual and his/her ability to "control."

There are certain people who can control everything on their desk. They can control the elements, the typography, the photography, the retouching, and so on. They feel very much in command, because they are dealing primarily with inanimate objects. When you get in the area of television, you're dealing sometimes with 50 or 100 people, and you're dealing with directors, producers, cameramen, gaffers, grips, and it's a constantly moving target. It's a different kind of control.

Q: Are there situations where a print advertisement can have more impact than a television commercial? Do certain products or selling appeals work better in print than in television, and why?

A: There are certain products where there is really a lot of information to be told and where 30 seconds just doesn't afford the time to communicate a decent amount of information. Print is far better in these situations. There is also a reality to print that often corresponds better with a certain kind of problem than television. Also, I might choose print because in this business, when everybody zigs, you zag. You might get an awful amount of leverage out of being in print when nobody else is. You may be able to *own* a magazine because nobody else is there. You have to look at the whole spectrum of possibilities and not at whether these things are better in either medium as an absolute.

But television is the favored medium now. In fact, when people talk about advertising today, they rarely talk about print. It always amazes me. I grew up in print and I love print, but I talk about television. Television is very seductive—you have the music, the motion, and the beautiful cinematography. I can make you cry in 30 seconds, or I can make you laugh in 30 seconds. The emotions are much more reachable in television than they are in print. In print, though it's possible, it is more difficult.

Q: Does advertising "work better" with certain types of people?

A: I would think not, unless you get to the end of the spectrum, where people absolutely and rigidly hate advertising of all sorts. It also depends on the product. The man who might not be interested in the Chivas Regal ad might be interested in an ad about a Rolls Royce. My mother wouldn't be interested in an ad about an IBM computer, but she would be interested in an ad on SOS Soap Pads. If the product's right from them, there's no reason why advertising shouldn't be right for them.

Q: One often hears about informational versus emotional advertising. What do these concepts mean in terms of the advertising you create?

A: Let's take the example of the Range Rover ad, "We brake for fish." All that this message is trying to convey is that the Range Rover is extremely capable off-road. From an intellectual point of view, we could simply say that the Range Rover is extremely capable off-road. But to capture the thought in these unimaginative and prosaic terms is rather dull. However, when you put the vehicle in an unusual off-road situation—like water—and you twist the familiar expression of "We brake for animals," you are communicating the

same information on an emotional level. Therefore, it's much more disarming and memorable.

Q: Is the use of emotion, as you're describing it, to draw the person into the ad or to make the message that you're trying to communicate more persuasive?

A: Both. It's to draw them into the ad, to make the message more persuasive, and it must be relevant to the product. It can't just be a funny joke that has no relevance to the product—it has to come out of the product's basic reason for being. I believe in trying to make people laugh at your advertising, make them smile, make them feel something. I believe in that very strongly. It goes back to why people read magazines—they don't read them for the ads.

Q: Does the same description apply if we are talking about television commercials?

A: Absolutely.

Q: What is the role of the creative person in creating?

A: I came to prefer that a writer and an art director usually sit together, and, together, they come up with the concept, the idea, the headline, the picture. This team approach was one of the innovations that Bill Bernbach brought into this business.

Today, the lines of responsibility are almost, but not totally, blurred. Everybody writes and everybody art directs. What you really have is a team of two people sitting down and coming up with the ad, the commercial, everything. Every ad you'll see here at this agency was done essentially by two people, a writer and an art director.

Q: What is the hardest part about creating a print ad?

A: It's the idea—it's always the idea. The idea is the impossible wall to scale, always, until you do it, and then it's so easy. It's always that elusive goal that constantly stares at you through a blank sheet of paper and says it's impossible until it's there. It's always that. I'm sure if you ask any writer or art director they will tell you the same thing. It's terrifying sometimes.

Q: In terms of the creative challenge, is there a difference between consumer and business-to-business advertising?

A: No, they're absolutely the same. It's a problem with a solution, and if you know the problem and know who you're talking to, the solution has to be there.

Q: *Do you have a favorite way to describe the major components of print advertising and what they can do and how they should work together?*

A: What's important is that the ad works as an entirety. Another way to think about it is to say that there must be a beginning to every ad. There has to be a point on every page where the art director and the writer want you to start. Whether that is the center of the page, the top right-hand corner, or the left-hand corner, there has to be an understanding, an agreement, and a logical reason where you want people to look first. There has to be a logical progression to every ad. There has to be the place my eye goes first, the place it goes second, third, and so on.

Q: *What is the role of celebrities in print advertising?*

A: I believe in the use of celebrities only when they are relevant to the product. If you're going to use a 7-foot basketball star because you have a lot of headroom in your car, that makes a lot of sense. If you're going to use him to sell peanut butter, that makes no sense at all.

For the most part, celebrity advertising is borrowed interest. You don't want the consumer walking away from your advertisement thinking about the celebrity and not thinking about the product. The *product* should be the celebrity. Only if a celebrity is relevant to a product does it make sense to use one. The same that holds true in print holds true in television.

Q: *What about the role of humor in print advertising?*

A: If it's relevant to the product, humor is a wonderful selling tool. It's a way for people to like you, and I think that if they like you there's a better chance they'll buy you. But even today, humor isn't without its critics. It's very hard to do, and it's also risky. Perhaps because it's so personal, you open yourself to a punchline that nobody appreciates.

That's not only embarrassing, but advertisers can lose customers and agencies can lose clients that way.

Q: *Let me ask you about the role of coupons in print advertising?*

A: They're there for a very good reason. If you can get an instant sale, an instant customer, an instant prospect from your advertising, why not? I think you'd be mad not to. I think they make a lot of sense for a lot of products. A coupon is a way to buy the product, a coupon is a way to get more information about the product. Now what would you rather do if you had a choice—just build brand loyalty or sell the product and build brand loyalty? I would prefer to sell the product.

Q: *From a creative perspective, how do you decide on the size of the ad to be run?*

A: Obviously, this is a time when management perspective may be more important, but from a creative perspective, biggest is the best. Why share a page with someone else? The sheer square inches that confront you screens out your competition. There may be more efficiencies in smaller units. You may have a motivating reason to be very small, such as you have the smallest umbrella ever made and you want to highlight that point. Maybe the media corresponds to the creative idea. So bigger is not always better. But as a generality, I would say it is.

Q: *When is it time to start a new campaign?*

A: Hopefully, never. You always hear that the client or agency grows tired of a campaign before the consumers even see it. That's true all too often.

When you set out to do a campaign, a lot of people say, "This should last at least three years." For me, when you sit down to do a campaign, it should ideally last forever. There should never be, unless there are underlying reasons, any plan for this campaign ever changing. It should be built and manipulated to last forever.

Q: *Can you provide an illustration of a campaign that has been relatively timeless and how it has been modified from year to year to take advantage of changes in product or changes to market?*

A: Again, I would choose Land Rover as a good example. Although the campaign has only been running for not quite 10 years, it's demonstrated an enormous amount of flexibility. For example, when we first began working with Land Rover, it was a single product: Range Rover. It has now evolved into a three-product company, with the Defender and the Discovery. Each product has a different audience. Therefore, each audience must get a relevant message from that product, yet at the same time all the advertising must remain within the context of the same campaign. We've had to deal with Range Rover's price increasing from $30,000 when first introduced to $60,000 today. We've had to deal with a handful of competitors in the beginning to over 35 today. What allows this campaign to adapt to all these changing needs and keep prevailing in the marketplace is a sound fundamental strategy to begin with. The campaign has stayed the same, but changed.

Q: What do you see as the major problems with the state of print advertising today?

A: Everything now is beautifully packaged and very safe. I would rather see more of the extremes. I think we've had more great print and we've had more terrible print. We're missing a lot of the fire some of the ads used to have. Everything moves in cycles, and sooner or later the cycle has to begin again.

Q: What do the changes to television—the zapping, the audience fragmentation—portend for print?

A: Zapping and the 15-second commercial are probably the best friends that print has ever had. Anything that makes television less attractive to watch is going to make advertisers consider print more attractive.

On top of this, the emergence of special-interest magazines has made print into a much more exciting medium. It is also very helpful to an advertiser, because you are being provided the opportunity to talk with somebody with a sharpened interest when they go through the magazine.

Q: What is your favorite myth about advertising that you would like to dispel?

A: That we have this insidious power to manipulate people through all types of hidden techniques, such as subliminal frames, anamorphic pictures, hidden persuaders, and things like that. I am constantly amazed by the number of otherwise intelligent people who subscribe to that incredible point of view.

Q: In the fifties, Rosser Reeves said that the most dangerous word of all in advertising is "originality." Do you agree or disagree?

A: I disagree violently with that. Let me answer that in a roundabout way. Going back 15 years or so, the word "creative" was somewhat of a dirty word. You couldn't use the word "creative" without being followed by the word "boutique," like Doyle Dane Bernbach, that creative boutique. To me the word "originality" is synonymous with creative. And creativity is what this business is about. The only way you're going to get somebody to look at your ad, whether it be in print or television, is to give them the proposition in a fresh and original way.

Originality is everything. It's the way you draw people in. It's the information you give them. It's the product. And if the product is original, it sets the stage for everything else, because everything should come from the product. Originality is great at any one of these levels, but it's mandatory in advertising, especially when you have a product that is nearly the same as everybody else's. How can I get you to listen to the same information over and over again unless I tell it to you in a fresh and original way, especially realizing that you're not reading this magazine or watching television because of our advertising?

Q: One often hears of the concepts of positioning and brand personality or character. Could you talk about both of those concepts as they apply to your work?

A: There is really no separation between the two. A brand obviously must have a position, it must have its place, its niche in the marketplace, in order to survive, in order to thrive. That's imperative. A brand must have a personality, it must have a feeling, it must evoke some kind of a human response from the intended purchaser. And every advertiser must build a long-term personality for its brand. That goal is mandatory.

The position of the brand and the personality are inseparable because when you sit down to position the brand you have to think of what is the appropriate tone for your advertising. Will that communicate the feeling that you want people to have about the product?

Q: What advice do you have for new people coming into the industry?

A: New people should try to understand what advertising appeals and doesn't appeal to them—and why. They should keep a list of the advertising they like: jot it down, tear it out of the magazine; find out the agencies who did it; also pull out the advertising they don't like, and find out the agency that did that. As a practical matter, never work for the agency whose advertising you don't like or respect. Accept no rules, I would tell them, except the one rule: Anything goes.

Jay Schulberg
BOZELL WORLDWIDE

Q: Could we start by establishing a working definition of advertising?

A: From my point of view, advertising informs and persuades consumers to think about your product or service and, hopefully, to buy it.

Q: What does successful advertising do?

A: The first principle of advertising is to sell. Some people in the creative end tend to get that confused. And sometimes creative—in other words, doing good, or outstanding, or fresh, or innovative creative work—gets out of balance with the selling message.

What we want to do is fresh and unexpected work that is also disciplined, effective, and sound. The way that we approach advertising comes down to four or five basic points.

One is to develop a very good strategy with a meaningful selling proposition. Once we have the strategy, the creative work has to be on strategy, and the selling message has to come through. It should be executed in an intrusive way. That can be done with humor or charm or emotion, etc., any of those elements. The humor or the charm or the brilliance must reinforce the selling message.

Finally, the creative must reward the reader for reading and the viewer for watching.

Q: Could you describe the role that advertising plays in the total buying process?

A: It informs people and, done well, it informs them persuasively. Most people would not be aware of most products, nor be inclined to buy them, without being informed by advertising that they exist and that they fulfill the need of the consumer.

Let me use an example. Huggies diapers is an enormously successful product. Without advertising, people would just have a random choice from a number of superficially similar products. With advertising, the public is informed that Huggies exist. Taking it one step further, by talking about what the benefit is to the consumer, the consumer is in a better position to understand the less apparent, but not less important, strengths of the product.

For Huggies, the initial strategy or selling promise was that they helped stop leaking. The basic execution was built around the mother's embarrassment, e.g., a christening ceremony and the priest or minister holding the baby and saying, "Uh-oh!" to a grandmother holding the baby with the same comment. From an executional point of view, that's cute and it's charming. However, from a strategic point of view, it was wrong, and the brand was performing poorly. What we did when we got the account was fine-tune the strategy and then come up with a unique execution. What is the ultimate benefit? It helps stop leaking to help make *your baby happier.* That's what we changed to. Mothers who buy diapers don't want to admit that they're buying a particular brand due to a selfish motivation such as the mother's embarrassment—the original position in the strategy.

Q: How do you see television advertising and print advertising as being different and being the same?

A: They're the same in the sense that all good advertising has to be intrusive, it has to be noticed, it has to be relevant, etc. It has to do all that.

But the mediums do and can do different things. TV can create awareness more quickly with a larger percentage of the population at a lower cost. To do that in print becomes prohibitively expensive; it's almost impossible. However, print can inform better.

If one has a complicated message or where the consumer is spending a lot of money for a product, such as a car or a VCR or a television set, people want information, and you can get a lot more into print than you can get into a 30-second spot. So, where TV may create the awareness, say for a car, people want to read about what the car has, in my view.

Q: Do certain types of products or appeals work better in one of the media versus the other?

A: Yes. There's a general rule of thumb that if you're spending a lot of money for a product—again, a car, television set, a VCR—you need information. That works better in print. Years ago I wrote an ad for Sears color TV sets, which at the time was the third most expensive item a person bought—you bought a house, a car, and a TV set. I wrote a double-page spread, and it was a thousand words of copy.

The ad was how to buy a color TV from Sears or anyone else. People read it. It was a campaign by itself, and ran it for four years. It was informative. It told people what they had to know about buying a TV set and all that sort of business. It gave them a lot of information. You can't do that in a 30-second spot.

Q: Could you describe the role of the creative person in creative advertising?

A: Yes. Creative people have to be all-around advertising people. They're not just art directors and writers who sit in the corners and somebody says, "Go write an ad on Merrill Lynch or Excedrin." They get involved with everything. They get involved with developing the strategy; they have to understand a good selling proposition; they need to know what a smart strategy is. They have to understand all nuances of marketing and be able to monitor change once they create the creative work. No creative work begins until the strategy is identified and fine-tuned.

Q: Can you describe the difference between a creative commercial and an effective commercial?

A: Going back years ago, there were the Harry and Bert Piel commercials for Piel's Beer. Everybody loved them—they were charming, they were funny, they were good. Great creative work, but they didn't sell the product; either they lost sight of what their objective was and they didn't know how to fix it, or it was too late to fix it. Today I think examples of good creative work that sells are Jeep and the *New York Times*. They're creative in the sense that they bring the consumer into the advertisement, and once in, they're being sold on the product or service as opposed to just being entertained.

Q: What is the hardest part about creating a print ad?

A: One of the problems we have in the business today is that there is a whole generation or two now that has grown up on television and television commercials. There's an allure to commercials that's like making a movie. But with television there are a lot of places to hide. You go out and hire a very expensive director, a very expensive production company, and the film looks great. There are a lot of people who get involved.

With print, there's no place to hide—there's just the writer, the art director, and a blank piece of paper. And that's why it's harder to do print than to do TV.

The writer and art director have to sit there and face a blank piece of paper.

Q: How long does it take to do a print ad?

A: I don't think there is any set answer. It comes back down to what is the idea. Sometimes you can come up with an idea very quickly. Other times you say, "Oh, my God, I can't think of anything." You walk around and it can be instantaneous or it can take weeks or months, and then you're coupled with a deadline pressure and you have to come up with an idea.

Q: In terms of the creative challenge, is there a difference between consumer and business-to-business advertising?

A: I don't believe that there are differences. Actually, a lot of the business-to-business should be just as emotional as consumer advertising. Even though you have to present a lot of information, it still can be done in a charming way, in an engaging way, and in a way which gets people's attention. It does not have to be dry or hack or boring because it is a so-called rational buying decision. By becoming more consumer oriented, more benefit driven, business-to-business advertising is becoming more intrusive, more persuasive, and more emotional.

Q: Do you have a favorite way to describe the major components of print advertising?

A: What's important is that it all works together as a unit. The ad itself has to be intrusive, and that can come about in a number of different ways. While the headline or the visual is intrusive, they both have to support one another.

Q: What is the role of celebrities in print advertising?

A: Most celebrity advertising in my view is wrong. It works only if the celebrity reinforces the selling message and is on strategy. For example, Bozell created the Milk Mustache campaign featuring celebrities Naomi Campbell, Lauren Bacall, Joan Rivers, Kate Moss, Kristi Yamaguchi, and many, many more.

The purpose of the campaign is educational. Many women need to drink more milk for health reasons. They are not drinking it for the *wrong* reasons—fat content. The fact is, skim or 1% milk contain all the vitamins, minerals, and calcium as whole milk, without fat or less fat. Many people don't know this. They think all the good stuff is taken out with the fat.

The celebrity with a milk mustache is a grabber that gets people's attention. The ad is almost a poster. There are only a few lines of copy. The opening and closing lines reflect the celebrity's personality. Lines two and three contain a surprising nugget of new information about milk to persuade women to drink. Celebrities in the milk campaign are relevant to specific target audiences. For example, Kate Moss and Naomi Campbell are targeted to teenagers; Joan Rivers and Lauren Bacall, to older women.

Q: How about the role of humor in print advertising?

A: Years ago there used to be a campaign for Dewar's which I thought was terrific. It was humor in advertising; it was as if Tommy Smothers wrote an ad for Dewar's. Other than that, I can think of very few examples of humor in print advertising. Why don't we see more? I don't know the answer. I think it's a fascinating question. Part of it may be that it's hard to keep it fresh. The humor that is there is not a "ha-ha," it's more of a warm type of a thing, the Snoopy and Metropolitan Life campaign, perhaps, or the sophisticated uses in Chivas Regal.

Q: How do you decide on the size of the ad—one page versus a spread? Is that part of the creative issue?

A: Yes, and it comes from two things. One is obviously the amount of money the client has to spend and then, beyond that, what is the largest size or the smallest size one can get away with and still be effective. I think one of the things we do wrong in the business is that people don't tend to make judgments on what is the most effective selling unit. One can often get away well with one-quarter page or a one-third page. Both the advertiser and agency can be guilty of a sometimes automatic reaction to go with a full page or spread. It's a temptation that should be resisted.

Q: When is it time to start a new campaign?

A: When the old one is not working anymore. One of the fundamental mistakes made in advertising is that campaigns change for the sake of change. That's one of the most destructive things imaginable. It's very hard to come up with a good campaign and a very good campaign that sells. And once you have it, you ought to stick with it and stay with it for years. What you do is try to keep it fresh and evolve it and, as I said, be able to read changes in the marketplace so you make changes and refinements in the executions and the creative work.

Q: I was wondering if you might be able to describe an example of a campaign that has been consistent over time but has changed also in response to improvements in the product or changes in the marketplace.

A: What we try to do is maintain the executional equity that we have, that we know is working, but make refinements within it. Let's go back to Huggies as an example, although it's more of a TV account than it is print. We start off with a very simple proposition, and that is, as I said, "it helps stop leaking to make babies happier." And then we did what we believe was a very unique execution within the diapers package goods category. We avoided the typical clichés most advertisers were doing at that time, which was basically having mothers and fathers cooing over babies mouthing copy prints. We opted instead for what were basically before-and-after demonstrations.

Some creative people make a mistake, because they refuse to change the advertising because they think it is just great the way it is. Conversely, there is often considerable pressure to throw out the old advertising and start over again because we have something new to say. Our solutions are generally to evolve the advertising. We seek out a way to read the marketplace, read changes in the marketplace, and to incorporate news while still retaining an executional equity.

Q: You increasingly hear the concept of brand personality or character. Is that a term that applies to what you're describing now?

A: All advertising has a personality—good or bad, prestige or schlock, meaningful or not. Jeep, for example, stands for individuality. "There's only one Jeep." So you're not going to do something that is out of character. A creative team can come up with a great execution, but if it's out of the tone and manner of the personality of that product or advertiser, it doesn't fly—we reject it.

A lot of it is not very good. On the creative end, we do not have enough people who are interested in creating great print advertising. It's improving, but their first disposition is to go to television. We have to get them away from that. And actually, some of the better people, some of the better agencies coming along today, are building their reputation not on TV but on print. Also, I think that many advertisers think it's okay to have theater, humor, or whatever the case may be, in TV. But in print we're going to tell the facts. And that's the wrong approach as well. To go back to the basic things again, make it emotional, make it provocative, make it interesting, make it benefit oriented. The same philosophy applies to print. I think all of us have to do better print.

Q: A number of people have characterized the current direction in advertising as moving from selling to serving and hawking to helping. What trends or directions do you see in print advertising as we look ahead from here?

A: I think that you will see a trend to do more intrusive print, more unexpected print, more engaging print, and more in print that rewards the reader for reading. You've got to get people's attention; otherwise, it's a total waste of the client's money.

Clients pay to advertise, but no one is paid to read an ad or watch a TV spot. As more and more people begin to flip a page or flip a channel, you have to find ways to get their attention without just shock for the sake of shock.

Q: What is your favorite myth about advertising that you would like to dispel?

A: That advertising forces people to buy things that they don't need. I don't believe that. The product can disappoint people, and therefore they won't come back and buy it again. But to say that advertising is an artificial stimulus and forces people to buy things they don't want is really to misunderstand the role of advertising and the individuality of the consumer.

Q: In the 1950s, Rosser Reeves said that the most dangerous word in all of advertising is "originality." Do you agree or disagree?

A: I disagree strongly. One has to have originality, and if we did not have originality in advertising or anything else, the world would stop. Progress would stop. We wouldn't be moving forward. We constantly have to be pushing the frontiers and expanding them. And that's what originality is about. You have to be disciplined in the way that you do it.

Originality—mindless originality, or something which is irrelevant or undisciplined—is wrong. But to

say that there should be no originality, period, is just as wrong. I think that's one of the things that went wrong in the seventies. It makes people slaves to the past and the formulas and the rules, and when that happens, progress stops. So one must have originality.

Q: What advice do you have for new people coming into the industry?

A: The same advice somebody gave me when I was starting out—he said, "work twice as hard as the next guy."

Q: What is your most inviolate rule in creating print advertising, and when should it be violated?

A: The rule is very simple, as I said in the beginning—brilliant, unexpected creative that sells brilliantly. This should never be violated.

Bob Skollar
GREY ADVERTISING

Q: Bob, let's start with a definition of what advertising is.

A: Strange animal. It's really a combination of art, science, and business. Advertising tells people something about a product or service and gives them some reason to say, "I'll try it. I'll try it once." After that, it's really the product performance that sells them. Advertising should provide that one little thing that helps people say, "I'm interested. I'll give it a shot."

Q: How does advertising contribute to the purchase process?

A: It's part of the mix. I am not a big believer in immediate persuasion—how, after seeing a commercial, a person says "That's it. I'm going out and buying the product right now." Sometimes when you hit it right it works like that, but usually a decision to purchase results from a combination of things in the whole marketplace. You start with the product. You have to have a valid product proposition. I like to think about it as a "telephone fact." What would you tell someone on the telephone about the product? What would be the reason you would give them to go buy it? That's about how much time we have, and it's one of the keys to successful advertising. You want to say something that's relevant to the person—that the person looks at and says, "Yeah, that's something that could work for me."

Q: Let's turn it around a little bit. Why do you think people look at advertising? What do you think they're trying to get out of it?

A: In addition to being entertaining—that's how you get someone to look at it—we have to offer up something that people want to know about. Now, sometimes what they want to "know" is an image. More often than not, what they want to know is a fact or factor that is going to affect the way they live in some way. They're looking to get some information—to find out more about what's out in the marketplace—new product, better product. *Why* they look at this particular ad gets into the crafting of it. How do we get their interest? First, you have to get them to look at it. I don't think most people start out by saying, "All right, I want to find out something about a product. Let me go through this magazine to see if I can find this information. I know I have to put up with the articles, but let me see if I can get some advertising information from this magazine." The ad has to grab them and say, "Listen. We've got something important or something interesting to tell you or something you may want to know about." There is no one way to do that. That's where the art takes over. Grab someone's attention, whether it's print or television, and hold them for a few seconds and get your message out there quickly and clearly.

Q: How do you know if advertising is successful?

A: The main measure I'm concerned about is sales in the marketplace, and even that can be iffy. Like I said, the best we can do is get people to try it once. For example, I've worked on Dominos Pizza. Like all restaurants, Domino's comes out with a lot of new products. We can do an ad and say, "Now we have buffalo wings," and get them to try it once, but if they are not good, they're not going to try them again. So it can be very hard to determine ad effectiveness. There are times when we're on-air and times when we're off-air, and sometimes you notice when you're on-air that sales are really going up. That tells you something.

Advertising can't take all the credit, but there is something going on there, whether it's awareness or whether there's something motivating people to cause them to do something. One of the interesting things about retail advertising is that you can know the next day if you have to fill up seats in a restaurant or if you have to get orders in a restaurant, you *know* if it's working or not. We also do research. We read the tracking data, and we get some awareness of that advertising and hear what people say about it. Often we test the ad in focus groups. But we also do something more quantitative. You look at numbers and you say, "Well, gee, a norm is 21 and this got a 24." Does that mean it's going to be successful in the marketplace? No. It gives you some guideline that says people are "getting it," whether they understand what the message is. Research can be a terrific creative tool. It's great for discovering real language and people will tell you if you're off or not. They may say, "I don't believe that a second." It can be tough for a creative guy to hear, but you can learn if you're onto the right thing or in the right direction.

Q: Do you have a case history you can share that demonstrates the value of advertising?

A: Kool-Aid. Kool-Aid is a product that's popular with kids, but it competes against some tough competitors like colas and other soft drinks. Kids like Kool-Aid, but there is "something" about Pepsi and Coke; they had Madonna and all the celebrities and, of course, your Mom and Dad drink it. So Kool-Aid had this nice little niche—a kid's drink—and we set out to see if we could even boost this up a little bit more through advertising. We created a campaign that tried to own its own type of cool—not a Pepsi cool but a kids kind of cool—and did the advertising over a couple years. Then a few years back we did a tracking study and we asked the question, "Which is the coolest drink?" All of a sudden we saw that Kool-Aid, for the 6–12 age group, moved ahead of Coke and Pepsi. Now, I can't say it's all because of the advertising, but it shows that advertising certainly helps.

Q: Turning to print, what's print for? What does it do?

A: First, let me tell you how I feel about print. I love print and the reason I love it is because there's no "cheating." It goes straight to the heart of the matter. In television you use great background music, do a great special effect, and get one of these terrific directors, and even the ugliest idea can become beautiful. In print, there is no hiding. You have to have it in basically a headline and a visual image. Either you have an idea or you don't. Now, of course, you can get beautiful photography, show a beautiful girl, you show a cute little baby, but it still turns on the quality of the idea. Another thing about print advertising is that it comes with the ultimate remote control. You're "flicking" those pages, you're usually not looking for the advertising. I've got to grab you on that one page. The other thing is that print is really the best writer's challenge. It's about writing. It's about language. It's about words much more so than television. Television used to be like a print ad that goes on for 30 seconds, but it's become much more visual and image oriented. In print, though, whether you use one word or long copy to get your message across, it really is very much about crafting language. Print is also used when you have limited budgets, when you want to convey information about a product or when you're trying to hit certain types of people. For example, you can reach working women a lot easier with women's magazines than with television.

Q: Can you convey mood and emotion in print?

A: I think you can. Look at a photograph, go to any museum, you can get emotion from what you see. There's no reason why you cannot get it from a print ad. And words, too. You get words in there that hit you right in the heart or the soul. Putting a quote from a child that creates a picture in the reader's mind is an emotional experience. It's a challenge. You don't have music or the sweeping shots of television to help you out.

Q: If you have a campaign that includes both print and TV, how do you like to think about the two media working?

A: They have to work together. Whatever a client does, whatever product we're working on, we're better off when we speak with one voice and have basically one message. We don't want to be unclear or confusing. Now that doesn't mean it has to be identical: a couple of clips from TV with a headline to it. But it has to be coming from the same sensibility. We think a lot about brand character, which is the way that the brand is perceived over years. It's everything other than the facts about the brand. What is my feeling about the brand, who is the brand? When I look at a print ad and I see a TV commercial, if I see they're talking about two different brand characters, I would never recommend that. Just as if I was doing four television commercials, I don't think they have to be "cookie cutters," but I think there are basic core sensibilities and message components that

have to exist across the campaign. I want you to hear one voice essentially.

Q: How does the audience to which the advertising is targeted play into what the advertiser says or shows?

A: It's critical. That's where you have to start. We can't do advertising for ourselves. You have to have a real sensibility about who our audiences are. Go and talk to them. Do groups. Talk to the people before we do the advertising. Hear what they say about it and what's important to them. I do a lot of kids' advertising. I think I'm able to do it pretty well, because I love being around kids. But it's very important that I avoid sitting around in a room with a group of executives saying, "Oh, kids will really like this." We do a lot of testing with kids. We show them print ads and storyboards. They will tell you very much if you've got it and will help you make it better. I'm talking about kids now, but the point is relevant to anybody. You have to know your audience. Some creative people say they're trying to do "cool" advertising. I like cool advertising. Sometimes cool advertising is the right thing to do, but sometimes it's not. It depends on who you're talking to, what is their frame of mind. If you're talking about something that's real important to them, if you're talking to a mom, if you're talking to someone who's making an important decision right away, "cool" is not necessarily the motivating word. It's understanding. You're trying to get inside the head of the consumer— trying to say something that is very relevant to them. To me, you always want their heads going up and down before you hit them with the facts. Is this your life? Is this what's important to you? Is this something you've been talking about? If the head is going up and down, you say, "Well, let me tell you something." If they say, "That's not me" or "They're not talking to me," if you don't nail your consumer right and not just demographically—really psychographically and understand what the head is about—the most fun advertising in the world, even advertising that wins all the awards, is not gonna really work.

Q: Is advertising becoming more targeted to the different psychographic groups, or does it still search for mass appeals?

A: Well, there are a couple answers. Certainly, there are a couple of reasons for saying it's becoming more targeted. One, media capabilities, both with print and television, allow you to slice the pie very thin. And it seems there are new magazines coming out every week that are very, very targeted. The other point is products. There are more and more products out there, and everyone's looking for its little niche. It's a totally different world than it was even five years ago. There are so many new products out there. Many are going after the same mass, but some are starting to focus a little more and trying to grab a particular group. The flip side of it is that there are a lot of clients whose budgets are down. Sometimes we do three campaigns—one for the kid group and one for the teen group and one for the adult group. Sometimes we've got to get a message that appeals to everybody.

Q: One often hears about rational versus emotional types of appeals or feature/benefit versus image kinds of advertising. What do these terms mean to you and are they relevant distinctions at this point?

A: They sound like they're different, but to me, the best advertising is a combination of both. I'll go back to my "telephone facts." If you've told me a fact that's important that I haven't heard before, we are pretty much there. Give it to me in the "right envelope," and I may be willing to watch the commercial or read the print ad. But most of the time you don't really have this huge product difference, and then it's a matter of positioning for image advertising or emotional advertising. You want to combine them both and if you don't really have that rational point, you look for something that at least is conveyed differently so that the consumer sees that there is a distinctive difference in this product. And then there is how you *feel* about the product, which can be as important as the rational fact behind the product. When you get into certain areas like a perfume or things like that, "rational" is a very small part, but positioning is very important. But image and emotion are not just a bunch of pretty pictures. It helps a person say, "I know where this goes in my world."

Q: Could you describe the process that you go through to create a print ad?

A: For me, there is no one method. Every person works differently, and I believe in whatever works. I don't sit down and say, "Now I have to come up with a print ad." I have the assignment and I start thinking about it. And I work that way until the whistle blows and I have to turn something in to the client. I do that with television and I do that with print. I like to think

about it and talk about it, and I may write something down as I first wake in the morning. I jot something down on a piece of paper, or I may be not thinking about it at the time—you know, I'm doing something with my child and I see an image. That's a great image and I say, "You know what. I'm going to file that someplace, because that works very well for what I've been thinking about here." And rarely am I only thinking about one thing.

Structurally, we work as teams and each art director and writer have their own method of working, but there's a time when you close the door and you start throwing around ideas. I don't like the hard distinction between writers and art directors. To me, a good writer has to think more about an ad than its words and a good art director has to think of some kind of message, words that communicate.

Q: You mentioned that you start with the assignment. What are the inputs that you start with?

A: I think most good creatives like the creative part of the process *and* the business part of it. I resent being handed the strategy. It used to be that a writer gave an art director a script—here it is, go draw the pictures. I feel kind of the same way when a strategy is slipped under the door. I work better when involved very, very early. When someone has a new product coming out, I want to talk about it. Talk about it not in terms of let's start throwing out some advertising, but what is it about, what we were saying before, where is the consumer on this? Unfortunately, we don't do as much of this as we would like. But it works better when we know more about the competitive frame, the way people are using the product now, and what they think about it, if there is any kind of personality going on, if they think about other than the rational side of it before we start doing the advertising. I like creative people to get involved very, very early in the process before the assignment is handed out, and then once they have it, have enough time to really think about it.

Q: When you judge a piece of print advertising, what do you look for? Do you look at the ad as a whole or look at the pieces? What do you think about the headline, the illustration, the body copy, and identification?

A: Anytime someone comes to me with advertising, I don't look at the advertising first. I say, "Tell me what the idea is." I want to make sure of the idea. If they say, "We have this cute little kid sitting on a swing," I say, "That's the execution. Tell me about the idea. What are you trying to say?" Then I look at the ad not as an advertising guy, but (as much as I can sitting in this office) I try to see myself as someone on a train reading a magazine. Am I gonna look at it? And if I look at it, what do I think or feel?

I don't think that any two people look at an ad in the same way. If there's a very stopping graphic, then that's where my eyes are going to go. If it's a big headline, if it's something that's going to grab my attention, that's where my eyes are going to go. If it's the product, if it's the person—I'm not big on rules except to make sure you have a focus on the idea and make sure that it's compelling enough so that people can become involved with it quickly.

Q: Some people think that it's getting harder and harder for ads to get noticed, for people to get involved with them. Do you think this is true, and what are some of the things in terms of print you can use to make advertising more compelling or more involved?

A: There's so much stuff out there that people are bombarded every place they look. This makes it harder to break through. Everybody knows that. That's a cliché. But there are things that help counter this trend. New technology in photography and broadcasting gives us more tools to use to make advertising more interesting. And while there are always people that knock advertising, when you do entertaining advertising, people like it and will look at it. I said it's becoming a little part of our culture. Advertising is a good information vehicle, but people don't go out looking for advertising to get information, but when it's there—when it grabs you—you say, "Oh good, I didn't know that before. I like that. I'll remember this when I'm in a store or I will ask a friend about it."

Q: You mentioned some of the new technology. On the print side, at least, how is the computer changing how ads are created?

A: I remember the first time one of our new art directors brought me an ad that he did on a computer. I was floored. What used to take weeks and had to be sent out could now be done in hours. But it's also a double-edged sword. Art direction can too easily become "What can I do on my computer?" So, what I've been doing lately is going back a little to the old days. I ask my art directors to bring me in the napkin with the idea on it. Bring me the image that you want to do. I get

nervous when someone begins thinking about an idea in terms of how to do it on the computer. It's great that you can go in and make an idea come to life a little bit, but it can't limit our creativity.

Q: How do you know when an ad's become stale and when it's time for something new?

A: That usually comes from our research people or from our account side. There are some things people like looking at over and over again, and some that have less a "shelf life" than others.

Q: There are certain devices that sometimes people use in print advertising to try to get more attention or more involvement, things like celebrities or coupons. How do you think about those kinds of devices, and do they have a role in creative advertising?

A: I don't like to think about them as devices, and they are two different things. Let's start with coupons because that's easy. If you've got a coupon for something, you use it. You need that call to action and, to me, the coupon is the ultimate call to action. We're always trying to build it into our advertising somehow. There are some people who will try the product now because of the coupon and others who will feel better about the product because of the coupon—both are "win situations."

Q: Are coupons usually part of the assignment or do they come out of the creation of the ad?

A: They're part of the assignment because that's a company decision. Celebrities? Celebrities are good if you have an idea first. I'm sure you can take an ad, throw in a celebrity's face, and probably get a little more awareness or recognition, but I don't think that's the way to use them. It should be a question of "What am I trying to say?" There's a person out there who stands for that, who says that, who will make people think about that a lot quicker."

Q: What advice do you have for people who are trying to get into the business, particularly on the creative side? What kind of training do you think they should have? What kind of abilities do you look for, and how should they go about developing their skills?

A: A lot of the schools now teach how to *think* about advertising and are very good at it. But what's most important is that you really have to like advertising. When I hire someone, whether it's junior or not, you can tell right away if they like it. If you want to be an artist, you should be an artist. There's plenty of room to do artistic things in advertising, but it is a very, very co-operative effort. You have to have strong enough ideas so that when people start chipping away at them, and it's going to happen I guarantee you with any account, you've got to bend but not break. The other thing is for writers, You got to like writing. It's not about "Gee, I got a quick, cool idea." It's very hard to get away with that anymore, especially when you're starting out, because very often you're not the one who's up for the next big campaign. Finally, print is a great way to do your spec book. If you can do it in print, you can probably do it in TV. And when they're doing a spec for a print ad, write body copy. I want to see if you like language. Do you know how to write conversationally? Do you have a flow of writing? Do you play with words? Most of all you'll need the passion. You gotta love it!

NOTE

Preceding editions of *Which Ad Pulled Best?* have concentrated on what might be called "general" advertising—magazine advertisements appearing in big-circulation consumer magazines or business magazines.

But in the last few years, "direct response" advertising has exploded as the fastest-growing type of advertising. Many general advertisers could profit from observing successful direct response techniques, and vice versa.

Accordingly, the following pages contain an interview with a successful user of direct response advertising. In these pages he defines the medium, describes some of its techniques, and points out how it differs from or is like general advertising.

Andrew Joseph Byrne
CONSULTANT IN DIRECT MARKETING AND
DIRECT ADVERTISING

Q: The most popular advertising medium for direct marketers is direct mail. Do you have any "dos" and "don'ts" on direct mail?

A: Yes. After you decide what you're going to say in a direct mailing, you answer the question, "Who's going to receive it?" So you're talking about mailing lists

And if you're making a mailing that actually *sells* a product or service by mail, you're wise to use "response" lists. These are mailing lists of people who have *bought* something by mail.

The other big mailing list category is "compiled' lists. These names have been taken from sources as directories and membership lists. Telephone owners and car owners are examples of large compiled mailing lists.

Surprisingly, even though a compiled list has demographics and psychographics very similar to those of your customers, it will practically never be as effective as a response list.

If your mailing isn't actually selling something by mail, that's when compiled lists make sense. You may, for example, need to obtain sales leads for salespeople. And enough of these sales leads must come in from particular territories. Response lists will practically never have enough names in concentrated territories. Instead, they're spread out. So, compiled mailing lists are the answer.

Now, here's a point that surprises people about direct mailings. The letter is the most important part of the mailing. I'm talking about a sales letter which should be used, not a weak "cover" letter which introduces the brochure. They are abominations.

The importance of the letter is a surprise to people, because the brochure might be four to six times more expensive. One explanation is that, while the brochure is "advertising" to the prospect, the letter is envisioned as a message from its signer, even though the same copywriter probably wrote both.

There have been tests made of a mailing that included a letter, a brochure, and a reply device. Fifty percent of a mailing list received the brochure and reply device. The other 50 percent received the letter and reply device. The "letter" mailing won. Incidentally, if the letter reads just like the brochure, it's a lousy letter. It should be one person talking to one other person. The "ours" and "wes" should be thrown out. There should be plenty of "yous" and "yours" and a sprinkling of "Is" and "mes," just as there would be in a regular letter a person would write. Again, one person talking to one other person.

Q.: How about a couple of "dos."

A: Okay. Here are a couple. Do prove your claim whenever you make one. Everyone makes claims. But your statements are believed only if you prove they are true. Support your claims with facts and figures. Use testimonials and case histories. Offer guarantees. And remember this: words like, "quality," "value," "service," and "dependability" aren't proof of anything.

Here's another "do." Do document the need for your product. Again, do use case histories, facts on the problem your product solves. Even though you may have proved your product is better than a competitor's, if the reader hasn't been shown that there's a problem, why should he [or she] be interested in your solution?

Q: A final question. Any recommendations on writing style?

A: Yes. Keep it simple, clear, and direct—short words, short sentences, short paragraphs. But I didn't say short copy.

Douglas Mueller of Gunning-Mueller Clear Writing Institute makes a great point. He reminds us that the *Wall Street Journal* covers complex subjects in language clearly understood by a junior in high school. Except for the front page. It's written to be understood by a freshman in high school. Other publications like *Newsweek* and *U.S. News* use identical standards.

Why so simple? Because research proved that the simpler the writing, the *more* would be read by their sophisticated, well-educated readers.

About 145 years ago, Nathaniel Hawthorne wrote this to an editor: "The greatest possible merit of style is, of course, to make the words absolutely disappear into the thought."

New York advertising executive Lois Korey observed, "The best print advertising seems to the reader to have no style. It's simply an intelligent, believable presentation of the facts."

The following 40 sets
of Consumer Advertisements
were tested by Gallup & Robinson

EXAMPLE 1

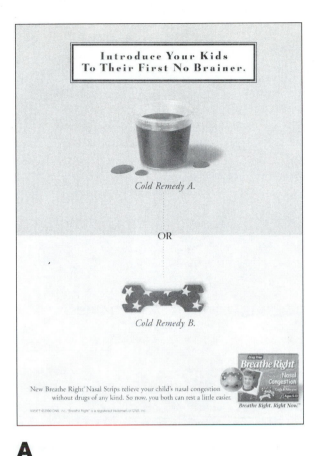

A

Introduce your kids to their first no brainer

Cold Remedy A or Cold Remedy B

New Breathe Right® Nasal Strips relieve your child's nasal congestion without drugs of any kind. So now, you both can rest a little easier.

B

Drug-free, instant relief from stuffiness due to colds and allergies never looked this good.

Spring-like action lifts open stuffy nasal passages. Look for them in the cold and cough section.

EXAMPLE 1

Size/color:	Both ads were 1-page, 4-color ads.
Test magazines:	Ad A—*People,* Fall Ad B—*Ladies' Home Journal,* Winter
Magazine type:	*People* magazine is a general audience weekly magazine for both men and women, focusing on personalities currently in the news, special events (Oscars, Grammys, etc.), and current offerings in books, records, TV/movies.
	Ladies' Home Journal is a women's service magazine, published monthly, covering stories and articles about beauty, fashion, home design and decorating, food and nutrition, health, and influential and interesting personalities.
Assignment:	Which ad performed better among women and why do you think so?

STUDENT ANALYSIS

NAME_____ CLASS_____ DATE_____

EXAMPLE 2

A

You're cold, you're wet, you've never felt healthier.

Tropicana Pure Premium Double Vitamin C with 100% E has the essential antioxidants that help maintain a healthy immune system. Now there's some news that's easy to swallow.

B

Your kids already love Capri Sun® in the silver pouch. Now it comes in a great tasting drink mix. So whenever they want, they can have as much as they want. And because it's from Capri Sun,® you know it's all natural. That's good news when your kids ask for more. And more.

EXAMPLE 2

Size/color: Both ads were 1-page, 4-color ads.

Test magazines: Ad A—*People,* Fall

Ad B—*Ladies' Home Journal,* Spring

Magazine type: *People* magazine is a general audience weekly magazine for both men and women, focusing on personalities currently in the news, special events (Oscars, Grammys, etc.), and current offerings in books, records, TV/movies.

Ladies' Home Journal is a women's service magazine, published monthly, covering stories and articles about beauty, fashion, home design and decorating, food and nutrition, health, and influential and interesting personalities.

Assignment: Which ad performed better among women and why do you think so?

STUDENT ANALYSIS

NAME_____ CLASS_____ DATE_____

EXAMPLE 3

A

Become a woman of the cloth

New daily facials

1. hold under water 2. lather 3. deep clean, gently exfoliate, moisturize 4. Have a little bit of a facial

It's the most extraordinary way to wash your face. With one easy, disposable cloth, your skin is transformed. Give yourself an Olay Daily Facial every day.

Proven to cleanse and exfoliate like a facial

B

so refreshing

facial cleansing

cloths

Alcohol free

Soap free

No greasy residue

Safe for sensitive skin

Cotton-soft cloths with natural botanicals remove dirt + make-up for a clean, fresh feeling.

(Clean refreshing tingle not pictured.)

EXAMPLE 3

Size/color:	Both ads were 1-page, 4-color ads.
Test magazines:	Ad A—*Glamour,* Fall Ad B—*Allure,* Fall
Magazine type:	*Glamour,* a magazine published monthly, is edited for the contemporary woman reporting on trends and how to adopt them. It focuses on beauty, health, personal relationships, travel, career, food, and entertainment.
	Allure is a monthly magazine edited for the contemporary woman of today and focuses on beauty tips and trends, hairstyling fashions, and feeling well.
Assignment:	Which ad performed better among women and why do you think so?

STUDENT ANALYSIS

NAME_____ CLASS_____ DATE_____

EXAMPLE 4

A

Create a flutter. New Longstemmed Lashes. Allergy Tested. 100% Fragrance Free.

B

Lancôme Paris

Limitless Length. Lavish Curl

Extencils

Dramatic Length Curling Mascara

Only from Lancôme. The patented prismatic brush and lift-and-set formula lift . . . lengthen . . . lock in curl in one extravagant step. For limitless length . . . lavish curl.

EXAMPLE 4

Size/color: Both ads were 1-page, 4-color ads.

Test magazines: Ad A—*Ladies' Home Journal,* Fall
Ad B—*Allure,* Fall

Magazine type: *Ladies' Home Journal* is a women's service magazine, published monthly, covering stories and articles about beauty, fashion, home design and decorating, food and nutrition, health, and influential and interesting personalities.

Allure is a monthly magazine edited for the contemporary woman of today and focuses on beauty tips and trends, hairstyling, fashions, and feeling well.

Assignment: Which ad performed better among women and why do you think so?

STUDENT ANALYSIS

NAME_____ CLASS_____ DATE_____

EXAMPLE 5

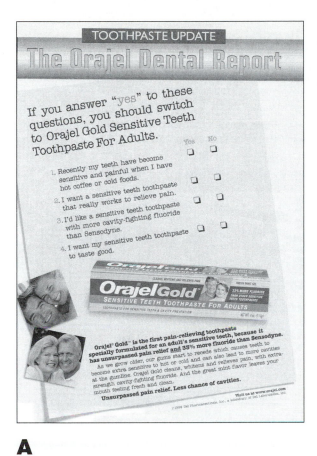

A

B

Toothpaste Update

The Orajel Dental Report

If you answer "yes" to these questions, you should switch to Orajel Gold Sensitive Teeth Toothpaste for adults.

1. Recently my teeth have become sensitive and painful when I have hot coffee or cold foods.
2. I want a sensitive teeth toothpaste that really works to relieve pain.
3. I'd like a sensitive teeth toothpaste with more cavity-fighting fluoride than Sensodyne.
4. I want my sensitive teeth toothpaste to taste good.

Orajel® Gold™ is the first pain-relieving toothpaste specially formulated for an adult's sensitive teeth, because it has unsurpassed pain relief and 33% more fluoride than Sensodyne.

As we grow older, our gums start to recede which causes teeth to become extra sensitive to hot or cold and can also lead to more cavities at the gumline. Orajel Gold cleans, whitens and relieves pain, with extra-strength cavity-fighting fluoride. And the great mint flavor leaves your mouth feeling fresh and clean.

Unsurpassed pain relief. Less chance of cavities.

I scream. You scream. No scream.

Clinical tests prove new Colgate Sensitive Maximum Strength Toothpaste delivers significantly more pain relief than Sensodyne. Our advanced formula soothes sensitive nerves inside your teeth, so the only sound you'll make is Mmmm.

Maximum strength relief for sensitive teeth.

EXAMPLE 5

Size/color:	Both ads were 1-page, 4-color ads.
Test magazines:	Ad A—*Ladies' Home Journal,* Spring Ad B—*People,* Summer
Magazine type:	*Ladies' Home Journal* is a women's service magazine, published monthly, covering stories and articles about beauty, fashion, home design and decorating, food and nutrition, health, and influential and interesting personalities.
	People magazine is a general audience weekly magazine for both men and women, focusing on personalities currently in the news, special events (Oscars, Grammys, etc.), and current offerings in books, records, TV/movies.
Assignment:	Which ad performed better among women and why do you think so?

STUDENT ANALYSIS

NAME_____ CLASS_____ DATE_____

EXAMPLE 6

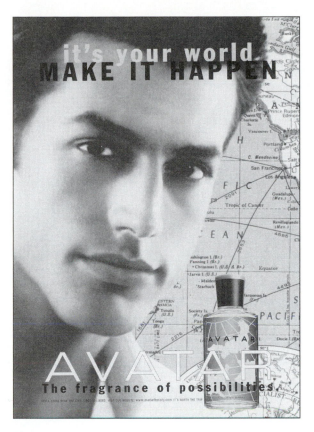

A

It's your world. Make it happen.

Avatar

The fragrance of possibilities.

B

Davidoff Cool Water

Available at fine department stores.

EXAMPLE 6

Size/color:	Both ads were 1-page, 4-color ads.
Test magazines:	Ad A—*Gentlemen's Quarterly,* Summer
	Ad B—*Gentlemen's Quarterly,* Summer
Magazine type:	*Gentlemen's Quarterly* is a men's magazine, published monthly, with strong focus on fashion, cool and current personalities, places, and issues, culture, money tips, music, some fiction, and current interest on staying trim and being at one's personal best.
Assignment:	Which ad performed better among men and why do you think so?

STUDENT ANALYSIS

NAME_____ CLASS_____ DATE_____

EXAMPLE 7

A

We vow to love every bone in each other's bodies.

For the calcium their bodies need, Josh and Karen wouldn't propose anything but milk. They're the winners of the Milk Mustache Mobile 100-City Cruise for Calcium Search, chosen from over 80,000 people to be featured in their very own milk ad. We'll drink to that.

got milk?

B

Noah Wyle, M.D.

(Milk Drinker)

Want strong bones? Your bones grow until about age 35 and the calcium in milk helps. After that, it helps keep them strong. So drink up. Doctor's orders.

got milk?

EXAMPLE 7

Size/color: Both ads were 1-page, 4-color ads.

Test magazines: Ad A—*People,* Winter
                   Ad B—*Glamour,* Fall

Magazine type: *People* magazine is a general audience weekly magazine for both men and women, focusing on personalities currently in the news, special events (Oscars, Grammys, etc.), and current offerings in books, records, TV/movies.

                   Glamour, a magazine published monthly, is edited for the contemporary woman reporting on trends and how to adopt them. It focuses on beauty, health, personal relationships, travel, career, food, and entertainment.

Assignment: Which ad performed better among women and why do you think so?

STUDENT ANALYSIS

NAME_____ CLASS_____ DATE_____

EXAMPLE 8

A

Tip: The closest thing to coffee bar coffee without having to deal with somebody named Serge.

Great coffee for generations™

B

FYI: Great coffee for connoisseurs. And those who don't know beans.

Great coffee for generations™

EXAMPLE 8

Size/color: Both ads were 1-page, 4-color ads.

Test magazines: Ad A—*Ladies' Home Journal,* Fall
                                Ad B—*Ladies' Home Journal,* Fall

Magazine type: *Ladies' Home Journal* is a women's service magazine, published monthly, covering stories and articles about beauty, fashion, home design and decorating, food and nutrition, health, and influential and interesting personalities.

Assignment: Which ad performed better among women and why do you think so?

STUDENT ANALYSIS

NAME_____ CLASS_____ DATE_____

EXAMPLE 9

A

B

Disaronno Originale.

Italian. Sensual. Warm.

Light A Fire

Kahlua Colorado Bulldog

Pour 1 1/2 oz. Kahlua and 4 oz. milk or cream into a glass with ice. Add a splash of cola. Begin round one.

EXAMPLE 9

Size/color:	Both ads were 1-page, 4-color ads.
Test magazines:	Ad A—*People,* Spring
	Ad B—*People,* Spring
Magazine type:	*People* is a general audience weekly magazine for both men and women, focusing on personalities currently in the news, special events (Oscars, Grammys, etc.), and current offerings in books, records, TV/movies.
Assignment:	Which ad performed better among women and why do you think so?

```
┌──────────────── STUDENT ANALYSIS ────────────────┐
│                                                   │
│  NAME_____ CLASS_____ DATE_____ │
│                                                   │
│                                                   │
│                                                   │
│                                                   │
│                                                   │
│                                                   │
│                                                   │
│                                                   │
│                                                   │
│                                                   │
│                                                   │
│                                                   │
│                                                   │
└───────────────────────────────────────────────────┘
```

EXAMPLE 10

A

Introducing the precision control system.™

Control the unexpected.

Intrigue is now the first and only midsize car to offer the Precision Control System. Using revolutionary control technology once reserved for marquees like Mercedes and BMW, the Precision Control System helps Intrigue faithfully follow your steering command—leaving you and everyone else on the road feeling a little more confident.

B

Don't move. We'll come to you.

The new 2000 Mercury Sable has foot pedals that move forward or backward at the push of a button. So they're never too close or too far away. Plus a Personal Safety System that includes dual-stage front airbags and energy-absorbing safety belts. How else does the new Sable accommodate you? Click or call.

www.mercuryvehicles.com   888.566.8888

EXAMPLE 10

Size/color:	Both ads were 1-page, 4-color ads.
Test magazines:	Ad A—*People,* Fall
	Ad B—*People,* Spring
Magazine type:	*People* is a general audience weekly magazine for both men and women, focusing on personalities currently in the news, special events (Oscars, Grammys, etc.), and current offerings in books, records, TV/movies.
Assignment:	Which ad performed better among women and why do you think so?

STUDENT ANALYSIS

NAME_____ CLASS_____ DATE_____

EXAMPLE 11

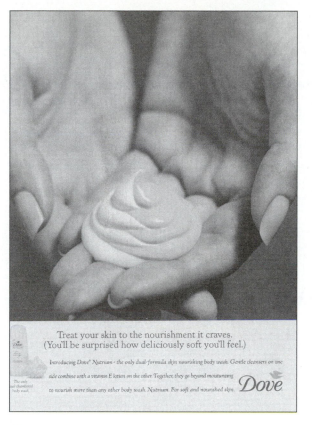

A

B

Treat your skin to the nourishment it craves. (You'll be surprised how deliciously soft you'll feel.)

Introducing Dove® Nutrium—the only dual-formula skin nourishing body wash. Gentle cleansers on one side combine with a vitamin E lotion on the other. Together, they go beyond moisturizing to nourish more than any other body wash. Nutrium. For soft and nourished skin.

With only hours until her wedding and her caterer missing in action, Kate felt amazingly calm.

Calm. One of the new Daily Renewal body washes in 4 transforming scents from Olay.

Proven to transform your body and your spirit

EXAMPLE 11

Size/color:	Both ads were 1-page, 4-color ads.
Test magazines:	Ad A—*Ladies' Home Journal,* Summer *People,* Fall Ad B—*People,* Fall
Magazine type:	*Ladies' Home Journal* is a women's service magazine, published monthly, covering stories and articles about beauty, fashion, home design and decorating, food and nutrition, health, and influential and interesting personalities.
	People magazine is a general audience weekly magazine for both men and women, focusing on personalities currently in the news, special events (Oscars, Grammys, etc.), and current offerings in books, records, TV/movies.
Assignment:	Which ad performed better among women and why do you think so?

STUDENT ANALYSIS

NAME_____ CLASS_____ DATE_____

EXAMPLE 12

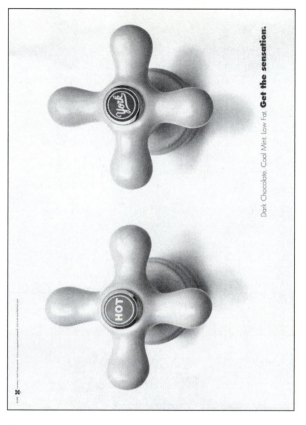

A

Dark Chocolate. Cool Mint. Low Fat. Get the sensation.®

B

Dark Chocolate. Cool Mint. Low Fat. Get the sensation.®

EXAMPLE 12

Size/color:	Both ads were 1-page, 4-color ads.
Test magazines:	Ad A—*People,* Spring Ad B—*Parents,* Fall
Magazine type:	*People* magazine is a general audience weekly magazine for both men and women, focusing on personalities currently in the news, special events (Oscars, Grammys, etc.), and current offerings in books, records, TV/movies.
	Parents magazine is a monthly magazine devoted to the concerns of raising a family, including the care of infants and young children, their needs and development; self-help in being a better parent; food and nutrition with timely recipes; health and beauty tips; fun time; and new products.
Assignment:	Which ad performed better among women and why do you think so?

STUDENT ANALYSIS

NAME_____ CLASS_____ DATE_____

EXAMPLE 13

A

B

Have a nice life span.

Get your soy with Silk.™
Everything your heart desires.

Taste and nutrition co-habitate harmoniously.

Get your soy with Silk.™
Uncarton the energy.

EXAMPLE 13

Size/color:	Both ads were 1-page, 4-color ads.
Test magazines:	Ad A—*People,* Summer Ad B—*People,* Summer
Magazine type:	*People* magazine is a general audience weekly magazine for both men and women, focusing on personalities currently in the news, special events (Oscars, Grammys, etc.), and current offerings in books, records, TV/movies.
Assignment:	Which ad performed better among women and why do you think so?

STUDENT ANALYSIS

NAME_____ CLASS_____ DATE_____

EXAMPLE 14

A

What's the simplest way to relieve children's allergies? (Lose the spoon.)

New Benadryl® Fastmelt™ quickly dissolves on your child's tongue.

All the allergy relief your child needs is in a little cherry tablet that quickly dissolves on the tongue—so there's no measuring and no chance for spills. It's the simplest way for you to treat your child's allergies.

Big Histamine Blocking Relief for Small People.

B

How do you get a kid with allergies back outside?

With Benadryl® The #1 choice of pediatricians for allergies.*

Allergy season is tough on some kids. But Benadryl will have them off and running in no time. Benadryl's Histamine Blocker blocks the histamines that can cause an allergic reaction to relieve the runny nose, itchy, watery eyes and sneezing.

Benadryl. Imagine Life Without Allergies.™

*Amongst OTC brands.

EXAMPLE 14

Size/color:	Both ads were 1-page, 4-color ads.
Test magazines:	Ad A—*People,* Summer
	Ladies' Home Journal, Summer
	Ad B—*People,* Spring
Magazine type:	*Ladies' Home Journal* is a women's service magazine, published monthly, covering stories and articles about beauty, fashion, home design and decorating, food and nutrition, health, and influential and interesting personalities.
	People magazine is a general audience weekly magazine for both men and women, focusing on personalities currently in the news, special events (Oscars, Grammys, etc.), and current offerings in books, records, TV/movies.
Assignment:	Which ad performed better among women and why do you think so?

STUDENT ANALYSIS

NAME_____ CLASS_____ DATE_____

EXAMPLE 15

A

You know a good thing when you smell it.

Innovate

don't imitate

B

Gucci

Envy

For men

EXAMPLE 15

Size/color: Both ads were 1-page, 4-color ads.

Test magazines: Ad A—*Gentlemen's Quarterly,* Summer
     Ad B—*Gentlemen's Quarterly,* Summer

Magazine type: *Gentlemen's Quarterly* is a men's magazine, published monthly, with strong focus on fashion, cool and current personalities, places, and issues, culture, money tips, music, some fiction, and current interest on staying trim and being at one's personal best.

Assignment: Which ad performed better among men and why do you think so?

STUDENT ANALYSIS

NAME_____ CLASS_____ DATE_____

EXAMPLE 16

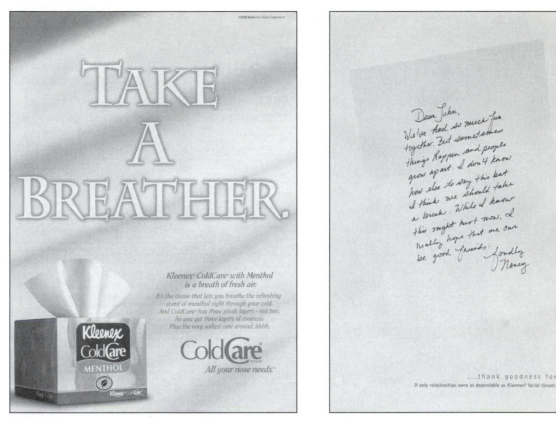

A

Take A Breather.

Kleenex® ColdCare® with Menthol is a breath of fresh air.

It's the tissue that lets you breathe the refreshing scent of menthol right through your cold. And ColdCare® has three plush layers—not two. So you get three layers of coolness. Plus the very softest care around. Ahhh.

ColdCare™ Tissue

All your nose needs.™

B

Dear John,

We've had so much fun together. But sometimes things happen and people grow apart. I don't know how else to say this but I think we should take a break. While I know this might hurt now, I really hope that we can be good friends.

Fondly

Nancy

. . . thank goodness for Kleenex

If only relationships were as dependable as Kleenex® facial tissues.

EXAMPLE 16

Size/color: Both ads were 1-page, 4-color ads.

Test magazines: Ad A—*Ladies' Home Journal,* Winter
Ad B—*People,* Fall

Magazine type: *Ladies' Home Journal* is a women's service magazine, published monthly, covering stories and articles about beauty, fashion, home design and decorating, food and nutrition, health, and influential and interesting personalities.

People magazine is a general audience weekly magazine for both men and women, focusing on personalities currently in the news, special events (Oscars, Grammys, etc.), and current offerings in books, records, TV/movies.

Assignment: Which ad performed better among women and why do you think so?

STUDENT ANALYSIS

NAME_____ CLASS_____ DATE_____

EXAMPLE 17

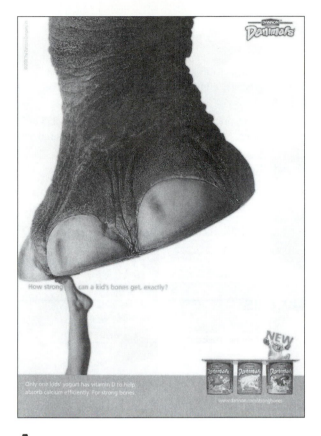

A

How strong can a kid's bones get, exactly?

Only one kids' yogurt has vitamin D to help absorb calcium efficiently. For strong bones.

B

Dangerously decadent.

Innocently all natural.

Breyers® Fruit on the Bottom Yogurt.

Tastes naughty, but it's not.

EXAMPLE 17

Size/color:	Both ads were 1-page, 4-color ads.
Test magazines:	Ad A—*People,* Summer
	Ad B—*Ladies' Home Journal,* Summer
Magazine type:	*People* magazine is a general audience weekly magazine for both men and women, focusing on personalities currently in the news, special events (Oscars, Grammys, etc.), and current offerings in books, records, TV/movies.
	Ladies' Home Journal is a women's service magazine, published monthly, covering stories and articles about beauty, fashion, home design and decorating, food and nutrition, health, and influential and interesting personalities.
Assignment:	Which ad performed better among women and why do you think so?

STUDENT ANALYSIS

NAME_____ CLASS_____ DATE_____

EXAMPLE 18

A

"I had a daydream about salad dressing. Is that weird?"

Not if it's Kraft® Special Collection. See, they've just intro-
duced two irresistible new flavors: Sun Dried Tomato and
Italian Pesto. Definitely the stuff dreams are made of.

Around here the dressing is Kraft.®

B

Help him help you.

Dress your vegetables in something good. New Taste of
Life™ dressings from Kraft are made with canola, high oleic
sunflower and olive oils. Plus, they're enriched with Vitamin
E and contain no saturated fat.

Kraft®

Taste of Life™

www.krafttasteoflife.com

EXAMPLE 18

Size/color:	Both ads were 1-page, 4-color ads.
Test magazines:	Ad A—*Glamour,* Spring
	Ad B—*People,* Spring
Magazine type:	*Glamour,* a magazine published monthly, is edited for the contemporary woman reporting on trends and how to adopt them. It focuses on beauty, health, personal relationships, travel, career, food, and entertainment.
	People magazine is a general audience weekly magazine for both men and women, focusing on personalities currently in the news, special events (Oscars, Grammys, etc.), and current offerings in books, records, TV/movies.
Assignment:	Which ad performed better among women and why do you think so?

STUDENT ANALYSIS

NAME_____ CLASS_____ DATE_____

EXAMPLE 19

A

So much about a family is revealed in its faces.

The New Family of Stainless Steel Watches.

Timex

B

The Timex Turn & Pull Alarm Watch.

More convenient than any excuse.

"Sorry I'm late for our date. My first date ran a little long."

"Sorry the turkey got burned. I got distracted by the giblets."

"Sorry I didn't pay the meter, officer. I only carry thousand dollar bills. Would you like one?"

To set the alarm, just turn the ring, pull the crown and it's precise to the setting. When the alarm sounds, the Indiglo® light flashes too. Use if for short-term reminders or for a daily alarm. The Timex Turn & Pull™ Alarm.

www.timex.com

EXAMPLE 19

Size/color:	Both ads were 1-page, 4-color ads.
Test magazines:	Ad A—*Gentlemen's Quarterly,* Spring Ad B—*People,* Fall
Magazine type:	*Gentlemen's Quarterly* is a men's magazine, published monthly, with strong focus on fashion, cool and current personalities, places, and issues, culture, money tips, music, some fiction, and current interest on staying trim and being at one's personal best.
	People magazine is a general audience weekly magazine for both men and women, focusing on personalities currently in the news, special events (Oscars, Grammys, etc.), and current offerings in books, records, TV/movies.
Assignment:	Which ad performed better among men and why do you think so?

STUDENT ANALYSIS

NAME_____ CLASS_____ DATE_____

EXAMPLE 20

A

Head Stand

You'll flip over new Glad® Stand & Zip™ bags. With their sturdy plastic and wide-pleated bottoms, they stand up all by themselves for easy filling, storing and snacking.

If other bags let you down

Don't Get Mad. Get Glad.™

B

Hard.

EZ.

The new Ziploc® EZ-Fill™ Bag in a one-of-a-kind tall size. Stands up tall. Stays open. Closes Ziploc tight. Also available in new $1/2$ gallon size.

EXAMPLE 20

Size/color: Both ads were 1-page, 4-color ads.

Test magazines: Ad A—*Bon Appetit,* Winter
                       Ad B—*Ladies' Home Journal,* Summer

Magazine type: *Bon Appetit* is a magazine published monthly. *Bon Appetit* focuses on sophisticated home entertaining with emphasis on food and its preparation, as well as travel, restaurants, hotels, inns, fine tableware, kitchen design, wines and spirits, and health and nutrition.

                       Ladies' Home Journal is a women's service magazine, published monthly, covering stories and articles about beauty, fashion, home design and decorating, food and nutrition, health, and influential and interesting personalities.

Assignment: Which ad performed better among women and why do you think so?

STUDENT ANALYSIS

NAME_____ CLASS_____ DATE_____

EXAMPLE 21

A

Viagra®

(sildenafil citrate) tablets

Let the dance begin.

B

Wishing You a Happy Valentine's Day

Viagra®

(sildenafil citrate) tablets

An "official sponsor" of Valentine's Day

EXAMPLE 21

Size/color:	Both ads were 1-page, 4-color ads.
Test magazines:	Ad A—*Ladies' Home Journal,* Spring Ad B—*People,* Winter
Magazine type:	*Ladies' Home Journal* is a women's service magazine, published monthly, covering stories and articles about beauty, fashion, home design and decorating, food and nutrition, health, and influential and interesting personalities.
	People magazine is a general audience weekly magazine for both men and women, focusing on personalities currently in the news, special events (Oscars, Grammys, etc.), and current offerings in books, records, TV/movies.
Assignment:	Which ad performed better among women and why do you think so?

STUDENT ANALYSIS

NAME_____ CLASS_____ DATE_____

EXAMPLE 22

A

Just Born! Give A Cheer!

The Driest of Diapers Is Finally Here.

Huggies® makes the driest diapers of them all. Like improved Huggies® Supreme. The exclusive BreatheDry™ System of layers now lets twice as much fresh air get in to help keep skin drier. And Fresh air is nature's way of keeping skin dry and healthy. It's one beautiful diaper for one beautiful baby—yours.

The Ultimate in Care.™

B

What's the winter forecast?

Snow, sleet and diaper rash.

It's rash season. When more babies get more diaper rash than any other time of year. Why now? Colds, flu and antibiotics, for starters. So be prepared with the first and only diaper specially designed to help treat and protect against diaper rash.

Pamper the winter skin they're in.

EXAMPLE 22

Size/color:	Both ads were 1-page, 4-color ads.
Test magazines:	Ad A—*People,* Winter *Parents,* Spring Ad B—*Parents,* Winter *People,* Winter
Magazine type:	*People* magazine is a general audience weekly magazine for both men and women, focusing on personalities currently in the news, special events (Oscars, Grammys, etc.), and current offerings in books, records, TV/movies.
	Parents magazine is a monthly magazine devoted to the concerns of raising a family, including the care of infants and young children, their needs and development; self-help in being a better parent; food and nutrition with timely recipes; health and beauty tips; fun time; and new products.
Assignment:	Which ad performed better among women and why do you think so?

STUDENT ANALYSIS

NAME_____ CLASS_____ DATE_____

EXAMPLE 23

A

Pucker Power

Scope

Cool Peppermint

Feel the tingle

Nothing kills more bad breath germs.

B

Aroma-Therapy

for couples

Scope

Original Mint

Feel the tingle

Nothing kills more bad breath germs.

EXAMPLE 23

Size/color:	Both ads were 1-page, 4-color ads.
Test magazines:	Ad A—*Glamour,* Winter
	Cosmopolitan, Winter
	Ad B—*Parents,* Winter
Magazine type:	*Glamour,* a magazine published monthly, is edited for the contemporary woman reporting on trends and how to adopt them. It focuses on beauty, health, personal relationships, travel, career, and food and entertainment.
	Cosmopolitan is a magazine published monthly, edited for the contemporary woman of today with emphasis on the emotional side of their lives. Topics include relationships, careers, beauty, fashion, as well as money, travel, and celebrity profiles.
	Parents magazine is a monthly magazine devoted to the concerns of raising a family, including the care of infants and young children, their needs and development; self-help in being a better parent; food and nutrition with timely recipes; health and beauty tips; fun time; and new products.
Assignment:	Which ad performed better among women and why do you think so?

STUDENT ANALYSIS

NAME_____ CLASS_____ DATE_____

EXAMPLE 24

A

We Can Do It!

Tampax was there.

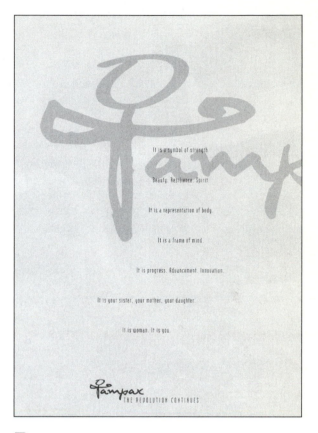

B

It is a symbol of strength. Beauty. Resilience. Spirit. It is a representation of body. It is a frame of mind. It is progress. Advancement. Innovation. It is your sister, your mother, your daughter. It is woman. It is you.

Tampax

The revolution continues.

EXAMPLE 24

Size/color:	Both ads were 1-page, 4-color ads.
Test magazines:	Ad A—*Glamour,* Spring
	Cosmopolitan, Winter
	Ad B—*People,* Summer
Magazine type:	*Glamour,* a magazine published monthly, is edited for the contemporary woman reporting on trends and how to adopt them. It focuses on beauty, health, personal relationships, travel, career, and food and entertainment.
	Cosmopolitan is a magazine published monthly, edited for the contemporary woman of today with emphasis on the emotional side of their lives. Topics include relationships, careers, beauty, fashion, as well as money, travel, and celebrity profiles.
	People magazine is a general audience weekly magazine for both men and women, focusing on personalities currently in the news, special events (Oscars, Grammys, etc.), and current offerings in books, records, TV/movies.
Assignment:	Which ad performed better among women and why do you think so?

STUDENT ANALYSIS

NAME_____ CLASS_____ DATE_____

EXAMPLE 25

A

Now soothe away long-lasting eye make-up.

New Nivea Visage eye make-up remover. You've never felt anything like it. A gentle gel-cream with therapeutic Pro-Vitamin B5. Not too heavy. Not too light. Yet it dissolves long-lasting eye make-up away without a trace, leaving you feeling soothed and soft.

Nivea brings your face to life.™

B

Wow!

Introducing Pond's™ cleansing & make-up remover towelettes

So revolutionary

Our dirt loving fiber gently cleans dirt, removes make-up in one easy step (even the dreaded waterproof kind)

So quick

Skin is left soft, healthy, clean in seconds.

EXAMPLE 25

Size/color:	Both ads were 1-page, 4-color ads.
Test magazines:	Ad A—*Allure,* Fall
	Ad B—*Ladies' Home Journal,* Winter;
	Glamour, Winter; *People,* Winter

Magazine type:

Allure is a monthly magazine edited for the contemporary woman of today and focuses on beauty tips and trends, hairstyling, fashions, and feeling well.

Ladies' Home Journal is a women's service magazine, published monthly, covering stories and articles about beauty, fashion, home design and decorating, food and nutrition, health, and influential and interesting personalities.

Glamour, a magazine published monthly, is edited for the contemporary woman reporting on trends and how to adopt them. It focuses on beauty, health, personal relationships, travel, career, and food and entertainment.

People magazine is a general audience weekly magazine for both men and women, focusing on personalities currently in the news, special events (Oscars, Grammys, etc.), and current offerings in books, records, TV/movies.

Assignment: Which ad performed better among women and why do you think so?

STUDENT ANALYSIS

NAME_____ CLASS_____ DATE_____

EXAMPLE 26

A

Why use this expensive anti-perspirant when Suave® works just as well?

Suave

Don't you look smart.

B

Softness:

Secret platinum protection.

Our Most

The most powerful form of protection you can get without a prescription

Surprising

is also mild. It's comforting

lotion respects your skin.

Strength.

Nothing is stronger.

Strong enough for a man, but made for you.

EXAMPLE 26

Size/color:	Both ads were 1-page, 4-color ads.
Test magazines:	Ad A—*People,* Summer
	Ad B—*Parents,* Winter
Magazine type:	*People* magazine is a general audience weekly magazine for both men and women, focusing on personalities currently in the news, special events (Oscars, Grammys, etc.), and current offerings in books, records, TV/movies.
	Parents magazine is a monthly magazine devoted to the concerns of raising a family, including the care of infants and young children, their needs and development; self-help in being a better parent; food and nutrition with timely recipes; health and beauty tips; fun time; and new products.
Assignment:	Which ad performed better among women and why do you think so?

STUDENT ANALYSIS

NAME_____ CLASS_____ DATE_____

EXAMPLE 27

 A

B

99⁴⁴/₁₀₀% pure beautiful

"Inside of me lives a little girl who was fierce and bold and completely free. Now I'm the one people depend on. But that little girl . . . I know she's still there, because I'll always be an Ivory® girl. That's Ivory. Still 99⁴⁴/₁₀₀% pure.® Pure clean. Pure beautiful. Pure me."

Forever fresh. Classic Ivory clean. Ivory soap

How will sensitive skin react to this antibacterial soap? It won't.

Introducing Sensitive Skin Dial. Hypoallergenic, no heavy dyes or perfumes. And still the most trusted antibacterial protection of all.

Dial clean. Doesn't that feel better?

EXAMPLE 27

Size/color:	Both ads were 1-page, 4-color ads.
Test magazines:	Ad A—*Glamour,* Winter Ad B—*Ladies' Home Journal,* Fall
Magazine type:	*Glamour,* a magazine published monthly, is edited for the contemporary woman reporting on trends and how to adopt them. It focuses on beauty, health, personal relationships, travel, career, and food and entertainment.
	Ladies' Home Journal is a women's service magazine, published monthly, covering stories and articles about beauty, fashion, home design and decorating, food and nutrition, health, and influential and interesting personalities.
Assignment:	Which ad performed better among women and why do you think so?

STUDENT ANALYSIS

NAME_____ CLASS_____ DATE_____

EXAMPLE 28

A

Discover Willow Lake. Let Earth mother your hair with soothing formulas and fragrances made from flowers and herbs.

Willow Lake®

Nature's Prescription for Beautiful Hair.™

B

Rain on me.

White Rain shampoo. Pure and simple.

White Rain®

Spend time in the rain.

EXAMPLE 28

Size/color:	Both ads were 1-page, 4-color ads.
Test magazines:	Ad A—*Glamour,* Spring Ad B—*Glamour,* Fall *People,* Fall
Magazine type:	*Glamour,* a magazine published monthly, is edited for the contemporary woman reporting on trends and how to adopt them. It focuses on beauty, health, personal relationships, travel, career, and food and entertainment.
	People magazine is a general audience weekly magazine for both men and women, focusing on personalities currently in the news, special events (Oscars, Grammys, etc.), and current offerings in books, records, TV/movies.
Assignment:	Which ad performed better among women and why do you think so?

STUDENT ANALYSIS

NAME_____ CLASS_____ DATE_____

EXAMPLE 29

A

You've been dreaming about your wedding all your life. Now it's time to begin planning.

You imagined what your wedding would be like. You just never imagined there would be so much to do. We're here to help, with interactive planning tools, useful advice, and thousands of bridal fashions right at your fingertips. We can even help you create your own wedding web site where friends and family can share the details of your wedding and browse your gift registry without ever setting foot in a mall. What it all adds up to is the Internet's most comprehensive wedding planning resource. And more importantly, the wedding of your dreams.

B

Gift Idea: Bowls

It's on their registry, at WeddingChannel.com™

Featuring the bridal and gift registries of these fine department stores:

The Bon Marche | Burdines | Goldsmith's | Lazarus | Macy's | Rich's | Sterns

EXAMPLE 29

Size/color:	Both ads were 1-page, 4-color ads.
Test magazines:	Ad A—*Glamour,* Spring Ad B—*People,* Spring
Magazine type:	*Glamour,* a magazine published monthly, is edited for the contemporary woman reporting on trends and how to adopt them. It focuses on beauty, health, personal relationships, travel, career, and food and entertainment.
	People magazine is a general audience weekly magazine for both men and women, focusing on personalities currently in the news, special events (Oscars, Grammys, etc.), and current offerings in books, records, TV/movies.
Assignment:	Which ad performed better among women and why do you think so?

STUDENT ANALYSIS

NAME_____ CLASS_____ DATE_____

EXAMPLE 30

A

Sure, it's all fun and games 'til someone runs out of Miracle Whip.®

A sandwich just isn't a sandwich without Miracle Whip Salad Dressing

B

Sorry, Charlie.

A tuna sandwich just isn't a tuna sandwich without the tangy zip® of Miracle Whip.®

EXAMPLE 30

Size/color:	Both ads were 1-page, 4-color ads.
Test magazines:	Ad A—*Ladies' Home Journal,* Fall Ad B—*People,* Summer
Magazine type:	*Ladies' Home Journal* is a women's service magazine, published monthly, covering stories and articles about beauty, fashion, home design and decorating, food and nutrition, health, and influential and interesting personalities.
	People magazine is a general audience weekly magazine for both men and women, focusing on personalities currently in the news, special events (Oscars, Grammys, etc.), and current offerings in books, records, TV/movies.
Assignment:	Which ad performed better among women and why do you think so?

STUDENT ANALYSIS

NAME_____ CLASS_____ DATE_____

EXAMPLE 31

A

The taste of mandarin oranges squeezed into 10 little calories. Can't you just burst?

Introducing Jell-O® Sugar Free Sparkling Mandarin Orange.

This new Jell-O® gelatin tastes like the juiciest orange exploding in your mouth. And it's only 10 calories per serving. Now, that's news that sparkles.

For best sparkling results, make with cold club soda. See package directions for more tips.

Also available in Sparkling White Grape and Sparkling Wild Berry.

Jell-O®

Smile more

B

I could go for something Jell-O®

Punch up the flavor. Use juice instead of cold water. Pow!

EXAMPLE 31

Size/color:	Both ads were 1-page, 4-color ads.
Test magazines:	Ad A—*People,* Spring
	Ad B—*Ladies' Home Journal,* Summer
Magazine type:	*People* magazine is a general audience weekly magazine for both men and women, focusing on personalities currently in the news, special events (Oscars, Grammys, etc.), and current offerings in books, records, TV/movies.
	Ladies' Home Journal is a women's service magazine, published monthly, covering stories and articles about beauty, fashion, home design and decorating, food and nutrition, health, and influential and interesting personalities.
Assignment:	Which ad performed better among women and why do you think so?

STUDENT ANALYSIS

NAME_____ CLASS_____ DATE_____

EXAMPLE 32

A

Adjust to stun

Pull to adjust your bust

Lily of France

X-Bra™

Your secret weapon

B

A sensual revolution.

A bra that's there.

But barely.

Smooth. Soft.

Unencumbered comfort.

Discover it.

Nothing feels better.™

Barely there.®

Now at better department stores.

EXAMPLE 32

Size/color: Both ads were 1-page, 4-color ads.

Test magazines: Ad A—*People*, Spring
Ad B—*Ladies' Home Journal,* Summer

Magazine type: *People* magazine is a general audience weekly magazine for both men and women, focusing on personalities currently in the news, special events (Oscars, Grammys, etc.), and current offerings in books, records, TV/movies.

Ladies' Home Journal is a women's service magazine, published monthly, covering stories and articles about beauty, fashion, home design and decorating, food and nutrition, health, and influential and interesting personalities.

Assignment: Which ad performed better among women and why do you think so?

STUDENT ANALYSIS

NAME_____ CLASS_____ DATE_____

EXAMPLE 33

A

The Aussie Philosophy #4

To Thine Own Hair Be True.

Kangaroo Paw Flower, found in Australia and in Aussie Sprunch Spray.

Always, without fail, be an individual. Dare to try what's different. Like getting to know all 36 of our identity-transforming products. Take a deep breath and sense the Chamomile, Cherry Bark and Kangaroo Paw (relax, it's just a flower). And know that your hair is being gently transformed. And remember, Aussie doesn't test its products on animals.

There's more to life than hair. But it's a good place to start.

B

Vanessa Marcil

Actress

You can never spot the ones who use Head & Shoulders.

If Head & Shoulders leaves my hair looking like this, why mess with a good thing.

Changes dandruff problems into beautiful hair.

EXAMPLE 33

Size/color:	Both ads were 1-page, 4-color ads.
Test magazines:	Ad A—*Gentlemen's Quarterly,* Summer
	Ad B—*Gentlemen's Quarterly,* Summer
Magazine type:	*Gentlemen's Quarterly* is a men's magazine, published monthly, with strong focus on fashion, cool and current personalities, places, and issues, culture, money tips, music, some fiction, and current interest on staying trim and being at one's personal best.
Assignment:	Which ad performed better among men and why do you think so?

STUDENT ANALYSIS

NAME_____ CLASS_____ DATE_____

EXAMPLE 34

A

You can't soften every blow. But you can buy a better bandage.

Nexcare™ Active™ Strips bandages bend and flex as you move. They're great for tough spots, like knees and knuckles. Great for tough kids, too. They're water-resistant, and they even stick to damp skin. Be prepared. Get to know all our clever first aid products.

Nexcare first aid. Feels better. Is better.™

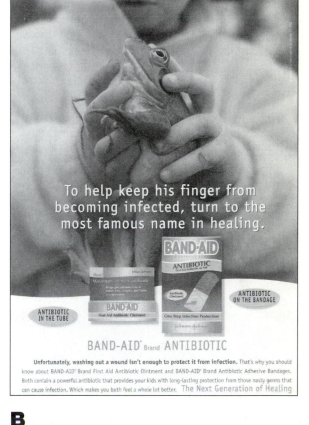

B

To help keep his finger from becoming infected, turn to the most famous name in healing.

Antibiotic in the tube

Antibiotic on the bandage

Band-Aid® Brand Antibiotic

Unfortunately, washing out a wound isn't enough to protect it from infection. That's why you should know about Band-Aid® Brand First Aid Antibiotic Ointment and Band-Aid® Brand Antibiotic Adhesive Bandages. Both contain a powerful antibiotic that provides your kids with long-lasting protection from those nasty germs that can cause infection. Which makes you both feel a whole lot better. The Next Generation of Healing.

EXAMPLE 34

Size/color:	Both ads were 1-page, 4-color ads.
Test magazines:	Ad A—*People*, Spring Ad B—*Parents,* Spring
Magazine type:	*People* magazine is a general audience weekly magazine for both men and women, focusing on personalities currently in the news, special events (Oscars, Grammys, etc.), and current offerings in books, records, TV/movies.
	Parents magazine is a monthly magazine devoted to the concerns of raising a family, including the care of infants and young children, their needs and development; self-help in being a better parent; food and nutrition with timely recipes; health and beauty tips; fun time; and new products.
Assignment:	Which ad performed better among women and why do you think so?

STUDENT ANALYSIS

NAME_____ CLASS_____ DATE_____

EXAMPLE 35

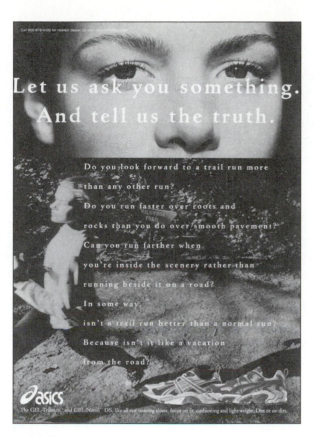

A

Let us ask you something

And tell us the truth.

Do you look forward to a trail run more than any other run?

Do you run faster over roots and rocks than you do over smooth pavement?

Can you run farther when you're inside the scenery rather than running beside it on a road?

In some way, isn't a trail run better than a normal run? Because isn't it like a vacation from the road?

B

Energy

Skechers.com

Free Catalog 1.800.201.4659

Skechers Sport Footwear

EXAMPLE 35

Size/color: Both ads were 1-page, 4-color ads.

Test magazines: Ad A—*People*, Summer
                    Ad B—*Allure,* Fall

Magazine type: *People* magazine is a general audience weekly magazine for both men and women, focusing on personalities currently in the news, special events (Oscars, Grammys, etc.), and current offerings in books, records, TV/movies.

                    Allure is a monthly magazine edited for the contemporary woman of today and focuses on beauty tips and trends, hairstyling, fashions, and feeling well.

Assignment: Which ad performed better among women and why do you think so?

STUDENT ANALYSIS

NAME_____ CLASS_____ DATE_____

EXAMPLE 36

A

"wouldn't you like a taste of power?"

let's talk

Avon color

Color is power and your Avon representative has it. Call your Avon representative right now for your free sample of new ultra color rich renewable lipstick with endless color bloom. Find your power color with Avon color styling. It's the rich, luscious color you won't find in department stores.

For a taste of power, call your Avon representative or 1 800 for Avon.

B

A Luscious Double Dip for Lips. New One Coat Lip Creams.

Fresh, Luscious Color. Rich outer core is fresh, lightweight color that wears for hours. SPF 15 protects.

Softer, Healthier-Looking Lips. Creamy inner core with milk proteins and Vitamins A, C and E super hydrates lips.

Hypo-Allergenic

Fresh Effortless Beauty

EXAMPLE 36

Size/color:	Both ads were 1-page, 4-color ads.
Test magazines:	Ad A—*People*, Summer
	Ad B—*Parents,* Spring
Magazine type:	*People* magazine is a general audience weekly magazine for both men and women, focusing on personalities currently in the news, special events (Oscars, Grammys, etc.), and current offerings in books, records, TV/movies.
	Parents magazine is a monthly magazine devoted to the concerns of raising a family, including the care of infants and young children, their needs and development; self-help in being a better parent; food and nutrition with timely recipes; health and beauty tips; fun time; and new products.
Assignment:	Which ad performed better among women and why do you think so?

STUDENT ANALYSIS

NAME_____ CLASS_____ DATE_____

EXAMPLE 37

A

Kellogg's®

Smart Start® cereal

Complex carbs

Essential vitamins

Key minerals

Great taste

Perfect cereal

Seize the Day™

B

Kellogg's®

Smart Start® cereal

Complex carbs

Essential vitamins

Key minerals

Great taste

Perfect cereal

Seize the Day™

EXAMPLE 37

Size/color: Both ads were 1-page, 4-color ads.

Test magazines: Ad A—*People*, Summer
                     Ad B—*People*, Summer

Magazine type: *People* magazine is a general audience weekly magazine for both men and women, focusing on personalities currently in the news, special events (Oscars, Grammys, etc.), and current offerings in books, records, TV/movies.

Assignment: Which ad performed better among women and why do you think so?

STUDENT ANALYSIS

NAME_____ CLASS_____ DATE_____

EXAMPLE 38

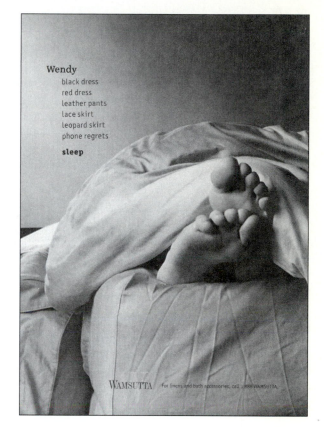

A

To enjoy a full day, don't spend your night with a flat pillow.

Make a durable DuPont Dacron® pillow your partner.

They say energy can't be created or destroyed. But it sure can be flattened out when you have to sleep on a flat pillow.

Lucky for you—and your energy level—DuPont Dacron® pillows stay twice as plump as those with generic fiberfill* We can't guarantee that you'll have twice the energy, but you'll certainly get a running start.

Now available with anti-bacterial fiber.

DuPont Dacron®

B

Wendy

black dress

red dress

leather pants

lace skirt

leopard skirt

phone regrets

sleep

Wamsutta

For linens and bath accessories, call 1.888.WAMSUTTA.

EXAMPLE 38

Size/color: Both ads were 1-page, 4-color ads.

Test magazines: Ad A—*Ladies' Home Journal,* Winter
Ad B—*People,* Winter

Magazine type: *Ladies' Home Journal* is a women's service magazine, published monthly, covering stories and articles about beauty, fashion, home design and decorating, food and nutrition, health, and influential and interesting personalities.

People magazine is a general audience weekly magazine for both men and women, focusing on personalities currently in the news, special events (Oscars, Grammys, etc.), and current offerings in books, records, TV/movies.

Assignment: Which ad performed better among women and why do you think so?

STUDENT ANALYSIS

NAME_____ CLASS_____ DATE_____

EXAMPLE 39

A

Study a cloud

Finish a novel in One Sitting

Enjoy something made Better With time

Slow Roast from Maxwell House®

Make Every Day Good to the Last Drop®

B

It's that moment when the world becomes still and the most pressing thing you have to do is nothing.

Explore the smooth, rich taste of new Swiss White Chocolate.

General Foods International Coffees®

It stirs the soul.™

EXAMPLE 39

Size/color: Both ads were 1-page, 4-color ads.

Test magazines: Ad A—*People,* Winter
Ad B—*Ladies' Home Journal,* Fall

Magazine type: *People* magazine is a general audience weekly magazine for both men and women, focusing on personalities currently in the news, special events (Oscars, Grammys, etc.), and current offerings in books, records, TV/movies.

Ladies' Home Journal is a women's service magazine, published monthly, covering stories and articles about beauty, fashion, home design and decorating, food and nutrition, health, and influential and interesting personalities.

Assignment: Which ad performed better among women and why do you think so?

STUDENT ANALYSIS

NAME_____ CLASS_____ DATE_____

EXAMPLE 40

A

Worst dressed gift

Best dressed gift

B

Introducing New Russell Stover Peanut Butter & Jelly Cups.

Gushing with Flavor™

For the first time ever, Russell Stover combines the world's most popular flavors; peanut butter, jelly and milk chocolate. New Russell Stover Peanut Butter & Jelly Cups—made with either Welch's Grape Jelly or Welch's Red Raspberry jam. The taste combination you'll gush over. Only from Russell Stover.

EXAMPLE 40

Size/color: Both ads were 1-page, 4-color ads.

Test magazines: Ad A—*People,* Summer
                   Ad B—*People,* Summer

Magazine type: *People* magazine is a general audience weekly magazine for both men and women, focusing on personalities currently in the news, special events (Oscars, Grammys, etc.), and current offerings in books, records, TV/movies.

Assignment: Which ad performed better among women and why do you think so?

STUDENT ANALYSIS

NAME_____ CLASS_____ DATE_____